"Your book <u>Walls</u> has been the required text for EdPM 199: Issues of Intercollegiate Athletes. This is a required class for all first-year athletes at the University of Oregon. The course addresses the current topics and problems relevant to intercollegiate athletes and teaches the appropriate developmental skills needed to successfully manage the pressures of being a student-athlete. The emphasis throughout this course is taking personal responsibility for ones actions and the decisions one makes as a student-athlete.

The book <u>Walls</u> has been an excellent resource for our students. It addresses each topic covered in this class and helps the students investigate their beliefs, values and walls that decide the decisions they make. The students have enjoyed reading the short chapters and have quoted your book in their Awareness Journal entries that they write each week.

I highly recommend this book to individuals for their personal use, as well as, a resource for the classroom. Jim, you have written a wonderful book to challenge individuals to look closely at their beliefs, actions and the walls they have created in their minds. Through their investigation, they can make positive changes."

Karen Nelson
Sports Counselor, SOAR Director
University of Oregon
Eugene, Oregon

"As an individual who has worked in human services for more than 30 years, I can state without reservation the WALLS Mentoring Program is one of the most effective tools to help users in making choices and developing a sense of personal responsibility. I have used the program, not only with our 16 to 20-year old incarcerated youth, but to train our staff and volunteers. Its reception has been uniformly positive from both groups."

Victor Brown, CAC, Executive Director
Adolescent Employability Skills Plus Program, Inc.
Albany, New York

"Jim Callahan has done an outstanding job in analyzing the what, why, and how we should view the concept of mentoring. He provides an original approach that allows the individual or organization to discover the power of the mind and how we all can benefit from each other. You will enjoy reading this book because the ideas are practical and purposeful."

Kevin D. Carr
Academic Coordinator
Florida State University
Tallahassee, Florida

"WALLS, in a sense, motivated me and cleared my mind on a lot of unanswered questions. It gave me a certain point of view and explanations that were different from those I received from my friends and family. I suggest that many teens read this type of book for information because they don't receive it in their homes. However, I think that the teens that are out there troubled really don't pay much attention or even care for the future. That is why we need to offer many different things, especially to those who want certain opinions for the future. Walls would be a good example."

Vera S.
Senior at the Franklin Learning Center
Philadelphia, Pennsylvania

"The WALLS program impressed me most by your ability to distill complicated psychological concepts into an easily understood format which could be applied to daily life by any reader."

Sandra Koss, MS, MA, CAC
Adolescent Employability Skills Plus Program, Inc.
Albany, New York

"Jim Callahan's <u>WALLS</u> provides an effective tool to help youth achieve a means of personal insight and furnishes them with an opportunity to evaluate alternative solutions. <u>WALLS</u> will help young people believe that they can change and that change is possible."

Robert Coughlin, Administrator
Ocean County Juvenile Detention Center
Toms River, New Jersey

"I find that the <u>WALLS</u> book is an outstanding conceptual presentation dealing with multiple aspects of success, centering responsibility on the individual. You have shared your personal journey of discovery in a very telling manner. With some additional structure, this would be an outstanding resource for new students in transition to college, seeking answers, strategies, and purpose."

Don Rosenblum, Ph.D.
Associate Dean for Academic Services
Delaware Valley College
Doylestown, Pennsylvania

"In developing the WALLS Mentoring Program, Jim Callahan has made a major contribution to the care of our children and adolescents. One thing we are sure of today is that youth's developmental trajectory is dependent upon the quality of the family and community environment. Families and communities that provide structure, good values, and an incremented movement toward individuation into adulthood produce healthier, happier, and more well adjusted people. Yet, particularly in our urban environments, many parents and communities lack the resources to fully attend to our young people. This is where mentoring programs for the youth and their families becomes a critical investment. What Jim Callahan has done is to develop a manualized approach to mentoring that makes sure the mentoring is of high quality. Recently the American Psychological Association had shown that health care programs which follow a well developed manual produce much better results than seat of the pants programs. Thus, Jim Callahan's mentoring program, Walls, is on the cutting edge of community health care programming. I urge you to read it and use it in your community, school, rehabilitation, or health care setting."

Ralph M. Turner, Ph.D.
Professor
Department of Psychiatry
Temple University School of Medicine
Philadelphia, Pennsylvania

WALLS

The quality of a person's life depends upon how you
create your reality guided by where you focus your
attention.

Life is made up of moments;
notice and enjoy each and every one.

BY
JIM CALLAHAN

Published by

Callahan Associates
P.O. Box 1472
Merchantville, NJ 08109

ISBN   0-9636270-1-5

WALLS

" THE BOUNDARIES WE ESTABLISH
FOR OUR MINDS ARE THE
GREATEST WALLS IN OUR LIVES."

I want to dedicate this book first to the memory of my father James J. Callahan Sr. I never understood the man, yet he was very instrumental in creating an environment which directed me to discover my own path and understand that I had to take responsibility for my own journey.

Second, I dedicate this book to my children. I hope it supports them in finding their path and enjoying their journey: my stepsons Erich and Scott and my sons Jason Christopher, Kevin Joseph and Christopher James

I would like to thank the following people for their support and help in the creation of this book: my mother Dorothy Compton, my sister Dorothy Labosky, my mother-in-law Phyllis Trahey, my son Jason and the following good friends: Nalin Jugran, Fraser M. Casey, Jerry Cable, Robert Daly, Joseph Belcher and Marie Hanna. I especially want to thank my wife Christine. Without her support and assistance this book would not exist.

Table of Contents

Forward

As you read this book consider this quote by Jane Garvey: "The future is not someplace we are going to, but a place we are creating. The paths to it are not found, they are made."

This book offers an opportunity for you to step out of your daily routines and explore issues that are basic to evaluating your choices and the meaning and purpose of your life. It is not designed to give you answers; rather, I hope it assists you in formulating new questions. New questions activate your creative ability to identify and evaluate new options. To assist you in exploring the issues in the book I offer "Thoughts for consideration" at the end of each chapter.

The book *WALLS* is being used as the focal point for interactive discussions among friends, in adult correctional institutions, juvenile detention, high schools, universities, and community groups. The interactive discussions expands one persons thinking and together the participants take the thoughts to a much higher level of exploring possibilities. (see: *WALLS* as a tool for mentoring, at the end of the book)

I often think about the old saying, "Good ideas are a dime a dozen. People who can make the ideas take life are one in a million." I hope you are a member of the one in a million group.

Considering personal development people fit into one of four groups. Nobody is in the same group all their lives and we do enter different groups at various times in our life. Sometimes we shift into a different group because of the event or situation at that time.

Group one: People in group one are stuck inside their walls. The idea of being responsible for their lives and exploring new options is outside their consideration. Some people in this group are living or existing in a very nonsupportive environment with little, if any, belief in a positive future. Other people in this group are so sure that they have the right answers that considering other possibilities is impossible.

Group two: People in this group believe in the possibility of new ideas which can improve the quality of their lives. These people have the ability to read a book, take the thoughts inside their minds, evaluate the ideas, and choose the ones that will assist them in improving the quality of their life. Most important, these people use the new ideas to make changes.

Group three: People in this group believe in the possibility of new ideas which can improve the quality of their lives, but they have a hard time just reading a book and using the information to make changes. These people seem to have more success evaluating new ideas in a group session. The dynamics of a group assist these people in bringing the thoughts to life. This may be a learned process because many of our learning experiences occur in groups such as school class rooms or religious services.

Group four: These people have problems that require professional help.

Introduction

The concept of walls and all the thoughts I have shared in this book relate to our journey from birth to death. This book is about living and traveling through this human experience, learning and expanding along the way. It is about the process of creating our reality and how we can take an active role in the process.

In 1933, Alfred Korzybski wrote a book titled Science and Sanity, in which he coined a statement, "the map is not the territory." The territory refers to the world we live in, including all the people, places, things, and events. The map refers to the understanding that each person is experiencing the world from his or her own perspective. This map is our current interpretation of the world.

For many years I have been fascinated with the process of how people choose to live and interact with other people and with their environment. Through observation, conversation, reading, seminars, and class room studies I have committed a great deal of time learning about the process of living from my own perspective and the perspective of many others. Each and every bit of information which I gathered affected my map of the territory, allowing my world to become a different place.

My purpose in writing this book is to first clearly identify and then share the world according to Callahan, in the hope of assisting each person in becoming the most valuable person they can be to themselves. My map may not fit into your reality; therefore, take whatever you feel fits and promotes growth toward a better map of your territory. Please do not take this process too seriously because we should dance with life and play with each thought as if it were a toy for our enjoyment.

I believe the most important person we meet growing through life is ourselves and this is the only person for whom we can accept total responsibility. This responsibility is something we cannot escape.

In grade school, either fifth or sixth grade, I remember the science teacher explaining the difference between potential and kinetic energy. She drew a picture of a lake on top of a mountain with a dam at one end. She explained while the water remained in the lake it was great for fishing, boating, and swimming and it also represented potential energy. She said that it had tremendous power which currently wasn't being used. She then drew the dam open and the water falling over the spillway with great force. There were turbines being driven by the falling water creating electrical power. The teacher explained that releasing the water from its potential state by opening the dam and allowing the water to go into motion, released its tremendous power, which is kinetic energy.

Everybody I have ever met has had some great ideas about how to better live his or her life and improve the quality of our world. People, like the lake on top of the mountain, often keep their power in the potential state. Success and achievement are obtained when we actively use the power of our abilities and convert our potential into the kinetic state.

As I write this book, my intention is not for you to read it cover to cover and then put it away. Learning, like living, is a participatory experience. I hope you play with each thought and then decide where it fits in your world.

Thoughts for consideration

If you do not trust yourself to take responsibility for your life, who do you trust to take that responsibility?

Consider each thought in this book and decide for yourself what you believe about each issue. It is good to disagree, but do not just pass by the idea. Instead identify what you believe about the issue or idea.

For each person nothing has any meaning or value except the meaning and value they give it. Consider what Hamlet said in William Shakespeare's play "Hamlet": "There {exists} nothing either good or bad but thinking makes it so."

Imagine you are preparing to play a new game. First you must learn and understand the rules of the game. Next you must identify and develop your abilities to successfully compete in the new game. Life is similar to a game. Identifying and understanding the rules and developing your abilities are essential for you to play and excel.

Are you willing to open your minds and play with the ideas in this book?
Who controls where you focus your attention?
Is life really a journey? How does this thought impact how you experience your life?
Is there a place in your life for improvement?
Do you deserve a better life?
Do you grow and expand each day?

Each night before you go to sleep think about the day and notice what choices you made and what other choices were available. Look for the small things that assist you in attaining the life you desire. Consider what you may do tomorrow to direct your focus and your life.

Wherever you go, you will find yourself there.

The first time I heard the phrase, "Wherever you go, you will find yourself there" was in a movie about Vietnam Veterans. One of the veterans had this phrase on a sign hanging on the back of his wheelchair. He liked the phrase because he realized that no matter how hard you run toward or away from anything in your life, you can never leave yourself behind.

I have known people who were having problems in their marriages and their final solution was divorce. They remarried and after a few years they were surprised to have the same type of problems that they had in their first marriage. The obvious problem is they could not divorce themselves and they brought to the new marriage the same behaviors they had in the first marriage.

When you search external to yourself for: purpose & meaning, happiness, love, self-respect, satisfaction, pride of achievement, and other similar qualities, you are searching in the wrong place.

A few years ago I read the following story:

An old man was sitting on the side of the road leading into his town. A man came up to him and told the old man that he was being transferred. He asked the old man, "What kind of town is this?" The old man asked the man, "What kind of town are you leaving?" The man explained that he really was glad to leave the old town because the people were unfriendly, rude, inconsiderate, and would never offer a helping hand to anyone. The old man said, "I think that is how you will find our town." The man thanked the old man and decided to look for another town.

A short time later another man came up to the old man, told him he was being transferred, and asked the old man, "What kind of town is this?" Once again the old man asked, "What kind of town are you leaving?" The man explained that he and his family did not want to move because the people in their town were so nice and friendly and would help anybody who needed anything. They loved the schools and their neighborhood and they had really great friends. The old man smiled and said, "I think that is exactly how you will find our town."

The old man knew that the town is the same for each man. He also knew that the men had different attitudes and views of the world and that they would find the town consistent with those attitudes and views.

chapter one

Walls

Travel with me back to the moment of your birth and remember the first interaction you had with other people. I cannot remember my birth and if the same is true for you, imagine the experience using what you know about the birth process. During the past months you have been in a soft, warm, loving environment with very little stress and everything you need for a wonderful existence. Today something different is happening. This great place is starting to get smaller and it seems to be pushing you toward one end. You don't know what is happening but you know something is changing and it is out of your control.

Seemingly this squeezing and pressure is never going to end when your head suddenly enters an entirely new atmosphere. Something is pulling you out of your home and you hope your head doesn't come off as you are pulled into this new place. Most of you is out, but these giant creatures are cutting off the part still in the place you have lived all these months. Now they are wiping you all over and sticking things into your mouth. At this point you probably don't appreciate this hostile place but you don't seem to be able to do anything but hold on and hope for the best.

Things finally seem to be calming down and you are doing okay. You are not as warm or as comfortable, but you don't believe you have any choice; therefore, you go along with the process, trusting things will work out. These giant creatures appear to have your best interests motivating their actions as they try to make you comfortable in this strange new place. You notice two of these creatures seem to behave as if they have some sort of ownership of you. This gives you a sense of hope and safety and you feel a little better as you close your eyes and rest.

Time moves along, as you will soon realize it always does, and these two creatures transport you to another place while making sounds like *home, mom, dad, family, and son or daughter.* Observing your new surroundings you soon understand you are somehow a part of this group identified as your family. This family seems to have a set of rules and expectations about how you should behave and what is appropriate for its newest member. This family apparently believes it knows what is best for you as it uses subtle feedback to direct you toward their schedule and beliefs. Sensing possible rejection you comply with the family's wishes and conform to their beliefs and expectations.

Time continues to pass as the hours become days, the days become weeks, the weeks become months and before long you develop into a child with the ability to interact with other people outside your family. You venture into the community where your family lives and you become part of another group called your neighborhood. You see another small child playing with a teddy bear which appears quite attractive, so you proceed to take the teddy bear for your own. Quickly you discover the society outside your family also has rules and expectations, and their method of enforcing the rules may not be as patient or subtle as that of your family. Once again preferring acceptance over rejection you learn and comply with this society's rules and expectations.

Finally, the big day has arrived: your first day at school. You realize this is a big moment in your life because you will be on your own, taking control of your life. Let me ask you a question. What do you think you learn on that first day of school? That's right! This new society, your school, has a set of rules and expectations which you must learn and comply with or rejection will once again be the order of the day. When you learn and comply with these rules you have happy faces sent home to your parents, but when you do not comply, the message home is quite different and unacceptable. Many times names are applied to you and your behavior like slow learner, passive-aggressive, learning disabled, or hyperactive. These names can label you for life.

The society we venture into can be as small as our family, or it can be our community, school, church, town, city, state, country, scout troop, or motorcycle gang. The reality is any time we enter a group of people, that group has a set of rules and expectations. We either conform to these rules and are accepted or do not conform and are rejected. Often we hear the phrases: *be yourself, find your own way, think for yourself,* and *be your own person,* yet the words seem to conflict with the understanding that we need to conform to the group in order to be part of the group. The words we hear don't always identify truth. Often we identify truth more accurately with our eyes than with our ears.

I believe from the moment of birth we are conditioned to conform to the rules and expectations of every society we enter. This conditioning is part of the process of socializing each individual into their society, establishing some sort of order, and avoiding chaos. What we often compromise is our responsibility to consciously direct our lives by our choices.

Some years ago I listened to Earl Nightingale's tape The Strangest Secret. Earl Nightingale tells a story about the great Albert Schweitzer being asked, "What's wrong with man today?" Albert Schweitzer answered, "The problem with man today is that man doesn't think." This answer really stuck in my mind because it did not seem to be complete. Accepting the idea that often man doesn't appear to think led me to question why not thinking is so universal.

The strangest secret Earl Nightingale identified is "You become what you think about." He also stated it is the strangest secret because it is really no secret at all, yet each person who identifies the secret believes they have discovered the magical factor of life.

These thoughts of Albert Schweitzer and Earl Nightingale caused me to further question why people do not think and why the Strangest Secret is a secret. This mental exercise constructed my belief that we are conditioned not to think for ourselves, but instead to conform to the external rules and expectations of our society. This conditioning process limits our ability to choose the direction of our life guided by our core values and standards.

This conditioning process leads us to create boundaries for our minds or allow others to establish boundaries for us. *The boundaries we establish for our minds are the greatest walls in our lives.* I use the metaphor of walls because walls not only hold you in but don't allow you to see out. Many times people stay where they are because they don't see or believe options are available. It becomes very difficult to move forward when you have no openings in your walls; therefore, people remain trapped within their walls.

Lets play with a puzzle I have enjoyed for many years. Below you will see a series of nine dots arranged in three rows of three. The goal is to connect all nine dots with four consecutive strait lines without lifting the pencil from the paper. You may cross another line but you can not retrace a line. For example, you may draw a square or a hour glass figure, but neither will accomplish the task.

The solution to this puzzle is quite simple and you can find it at the end of this chapter. While you work on the puzzle consider these two clues: children tend to solve the puzzle faster than adults and the boundaries we establish for our minds are the greatest walls in our lives. Seemingly, the process of conditioning individuals into society is very basic and important because we must cooperate with each other and learn to live together. We must also recognize every human being is going through the experience of living their lives. Each of us is traveling our own path from birth to death.

In terms of becoming the most complete and balanced person we can, it is important to recognize our relationship with others and society, yet we must also become aware and understand who we are as an individual. The process of socialization has the down-side of developing thought patterns which restrict individual thinking in terms of what is really important to our unique entity. The walls established for our minds by conditioning the thought process to conform, limits our ability to identify and evaluate our choices by our standards.

This concept of walls is not suggesting rebellion against all the societies we are part of; instead, it suggests we take responsibility for our choices and evaluate each choice by our standards rather than reacting according to a conditioned pattern or wall.

The word walls has often been used to indicate some protection from the outside world. Whenever I hear this idea of these emotional walls as protecting oneself, I envision an ostrich sticking its head in the ground when it senses danger. I always considered this a humorous and strange quirk in nature because not looking doesn't remove the danger. By hiding its head, the ostrich eliminates its ability to react and possibly avoid the danger. When people justify their walls as protection, they also choose not to address their fears or limiting beliefs; therefore, eliminating their ability to discover more supportive and expansive options.

Solution to the puzzle:

The difficulty most people have with this puzzle is they assume the square, made by the nine dots, is the boundary of the puzzle. You have to expand outside this preconceived boundary before you can draw four consecutive straight lines which go through all nine dots.

Preconceived boundary   Solution

Thoughts for consideration

If you are wearing a wrist watch put the watch on your other wrist. Notice how uncomfortable it feels and as you check the time do you continue to look at the wrong wrist? Our bodies often run patterns without thinking. Our minds also tend to run patterns without thinking and these patterns are some of the walls that restrict us from identifying and making different choices.

Will noticing our running patterns help us identify new options?

Some other examples of patterns are:

Which hand do you hold your tooth brush when you put on the tooth paste?
Do you move the brush or do you move the tooth paste?

When you put on a coat, which arm do you put on first? Try putting the other arm on first.

Clasp your hands interlocking your fingers. Which thumb is on the top? Reverse the position of your fingers so that the other thumb is on top. How does it feel? Most likely strange.

By identifying these patterns we experience our body and mind running patterns without any conscious thought.

Think of some of patterns you tend to run.

Often when labels like slow learner, learning disabled, or other labels which imply a lack of ability are placed on a person they tend to develop a self image that reflects that attitude. This self image surely does not get the person excited about getting up every day, especially when they are going back to the place where these labels were established in the first place.

Expectation = Self image = Performance

If we do not let people be responsible for their own choices, how can we hold them accountable for the outcome of those choices?

Do you think Albert Schweitzer was right in his belief, "The problem with man today is that man doesn't think"?

What boundaries do you have in your life?

What limiting beliefs?

Is it possible you have walls that you are not aware of?

Are you in control of where you focus your attention?

Is it possible you are trapped within the walls of your patterns?

Read the sentence below and count how many times the letter F appears.

FINISHED FILES ARE THE RE-
SULT OF YEARS OF SCIENTIF-
IC STUDY COMBINED WITH THE
EXPERIENCE OF MANY YEARS.

Count the Fs again. This time pay special conscious attention to the word "OF".

Actually there are 6 Fs in the sentence yet over 50% of the people will only see 3 Fs. Less than 10% will see all 6 Fs.

What happens is the F in the word "OF" sounds like V. Also as we learn to read we develop the pattern of not consciously noticing the small words such as of, and, the, a, an, etc. Our learned patterns have become walls that restrict us from seeing what is accurate and right in front of our eyes.

Outside-in vs. Inside-out

Lately, I have been thinking about whether I experience the world outside-in or inside-out. Outside-in is experiencing the world as it really is with no filters of my past experience. Perhaps a baby or very young child can be identified as seeing the world outside-in. The baby has not established any filters which can distort what it experiences. This may be one of the reasons we have the greatest amount of learning in our life between birth and

33

age three to five. Inside-out is when our filters of past experience distorts what we experience.

I believe we all experience the world both outside-in and inside-out and it is important to recognize which state we are in. Outside-in allows learning to occur because the greatest resource for new ideas for us to consider lies in the minds of people with a different perspective from our own. Inside-out seems to only reinforce our existing beliefs.

How do you experience the world, outside-in or inside-out?

Can consciously identifying which state you are in help you maximize learning opportunities?

chapter two

Human Paradox

When my son Jason was 14 years old, I realized the time I spent alone with him sharing new adventures was becoming less and less. The future would allow fewer opportunities because as the natural process of his growing toward adulthood progressed, he would do more things on his own leaving Dad behind. We decided one last adventure alone was appropriate and we headed to Cancun, Mexico, for a week in the sun. We were real tourists enjoying a great week of fishing, swimming, snorkeling, touring, watching bull fights, and learning about a culture very different from ours.

Touring in a country with a different culture and speaking a different language is quite a unique learning experience. I found myself observing the people and their environment, yet I didn't really become an active part of their culture. I was a tourist and I felt somewhat out of control because I knew their rules and expectations would impact on my activity.

This experience of being a tourist lead to the self-realization that in many areas I was a tourist in my own life. Much of my life was responding to events and activities controlled by my environment. The question arose: Can I be successful with my life always being a tourist? Answering this question uncovered a more profound question. What is success? Success seems to be a very personal concept and difficult to define. My definition not only identifies success for me, but also supports the direction of my life. *Success is living every day of your life in the direction of your own goals, dreams, and ideals.* Successful people are those people doing with their lives whatever they really desire. Successful people live their dreams. You are the only person who can validate your success because you are the only person who truly knows what you really want.

Being a tourist is all right for unimportant things, but we need to take conscious control over the things which impact on our successful living. Over the years I have committed a great deal of time studying achievement and success. Every book and theory I have discovered starts in the same place: goals. You have to know where you are going and apply yourself in that direction. Without goals or direction we are tourists in our own lives.

Our society often influences our choice as to what is best for us, and we buy into goals which may or may not reflect our true desires. Our self-image is often constructed by our winning or losing in our attempt to attain these goals. Our personal self-worth becomes dependent upon an event or series of events which may be established and controlled by other people. I believe too much emphasis is placed on winning and losing in our society. The only person who can make you a loser is you. Either you quit or you did not pay the price of preparing to accomplish the task. It doesn't matter how good you are at anything; somebody can always do it better, at least some of the time. Losing is something you do. Being beaten is something that somebody else does to you. Rather than focusing on winning or losing consider every event in your life as a learning experience. Each experience supplies information which allows you to alter your behavior and proceed more effectively forward, toward the life you choose.

Reflecting on my vacation in Cancun, I realized what was missing in my own life. I had never established real meaningful personal goals, the type which are capable of getting me out of bed every morning and exciting me about being alive and the direction of my life. I had become the ultimate tourist, taking each event however it developed, and making the best of each situation. Being a tourist isn't bad, yet I realized it lacks the personal satisfaction and pride of achievement essential for my successful living.

Sharing my new insights within my circle of acquaintances, I found most of them uncomfortable with the idea of being a tourist in their own lives. Upon further reflection these same people didn't really have clear concise goals directing their lives. Many of these people admitted they would like to achieve more in their lives but felt they were doing okay considering the times, the economy, their age, their situation, and so on.

Goal-setting is a rather basic and valuable task. The consensus of every book, tape, seminar, and theory of success and achievement of which I am aware identifies goal-setting as the first step to all achievement. Ironically, my observation is that most people don't ever establish these life goals. I offer again Earl Nightingale's strangest secret, "You become what you think about" (your goals). What causes this essential step of goal-setting to be consistently absent?

In the world according to Callahan this phenomenon is identified as the *human paradox*. The first step to any achievement or success is goal-setting. Goal-setting is simply identifying what you want in your life and knowing where you are going. Meaningful goals and dreams sufficient to get us up every morning and add excitement to our lives must be established internally at the core level of who we are.

Although this first step, goal-setting, seems basic and relatively easy, it can actually be quite difficult. Our walls can limit our self-knowledge and our perception of the world and its opportunities. My observation is we are conditioned to conform to our society, resulting in externally directed goals. Often these externally motivated goals lack the impact to affect our behavior. Usually when it becomes difficult, and it always does, we back off and forget these goals and once again become a tourist in our own lives. Unfortunately we also reinforce our inability to succeed. My belief is the human paradox creates and feeds conflict and incongruence between behavior, core values, and beliefs and manifests itself with the individual not being satisfied with their life.

Being a tourist is fine in dealing with many of the less relevant events we encounter in daily living. When our core values and the direction of our successful living is involved, we must be the captains of our own ship and consciously choose our behavior and the direction of our lives. Remember, we cannot control the wind but we can control our sails.

The only way I have ever found to really enjoy and appreciate the satisfaction and pride of achievement is to identify a goal consistent with my personal values and beliefs and proceed until it was successfully completed. All of my successes as a tourist, making the best of what ever came my way, left me with shallow victories lacking in personal satisfaction and pride of achievement.

When the games are over, and the day is done, I go to bed knowing the only person who can validate the satisfaction and achievement of my day and my life, is me.

Thoughts for consideration

Many people do not seem to have dreams, goals, or ideals. They have never actually considered what they want in their lives or what their lives are about. Without meaningful dreams, goals, and ideals we are just putting in time rather than living the life we desire.

What do you really want in your life? What is stopping you from getting it?
What are your dreams, goals, and ideals?
Do you deserve success in your life? If not, why not?
Can you be successful in your life if you do not know what outcome you want?
Have you established your goals based upon other people's standards?

I have noticed the term goal-setting has been used so often that sometimes people shut off communication when the term is used. Goal-setting is simply having an idea about what you want in your life. It is your anticipation of the outcome of your efforts.

Do you consider what you want in your life from your own values?
Do other people's expectations direct how you judge your own success?
Do you know what you want in and for your future?

Think back to a time in your life when you decided you wanted something, committed yourself to attaining it, and got what you wanted.

How did you feel when you got what you wanted?
Did you have to develop new skills to achieve your goal?
Did you work through some frustrations because things didn't always go your way?
Did the focus on an outcome add excitement to every day?
Did you have to re-examine some beliefs? Maybe do some things differently?
Did you have to "give and take" (compromise) with others to accomplish your goal?

Focusing attention

The following is an experience I had which illustrates that focusing attention on what is important to you can direct your life.

Before I wrote the book WALLS, I was a distributor of factory floor furniture. In one of my accounts there was a man, working on an assembly line, who always seemed uptight and unhappy.

One day I noticed him taking a break and I asked him, "How do you like working here?" He very quickly told me he hated his job because it was boring, mundane, and nobody appreciated what he did. He said if it wasn't for his responsibility to his family he would quit.

I asked, "Your family must mean a great deal to you?" He told me he and his wife have not been getting along so well lately and his relationship with his three sons isn't what he dreamed about. He was often tired and short

41

tempered and he admitted he feels he sacrifices 40 hours a week for the family, so he spends much of his free time away from the family, hunting and fishing. This was not his dream of a family because he had a poor relationship with his father and he promised himself he would be the best father he could.

I asked, "How would your life be without your family?" He answered, "Empty." He explained, "I loved my wife when I married her and I still love her, even though I don't tell her very often, and the boys are the most important people in my life."

I asked, "What do you want to provide for them as a father?" He identified he wants to be reliable and provide the financial stability they need to live in a good neighborhood and go to good schools. He also wants to help them go to college.

I asked, "Does this job allow you to supply those needs?" He responded, "This company pays very well, has a great benefits package, and even has a college assistance program for family members. It is also very stable." He also told me he never went to college and his education and training were lacking. He feels lucky to have a job with this company.

I suggested he bring a picture of his family to his work bench and when he starts getting bored and frustrated he can look at the picture and focus on the good things about his job. He thought it was a good idea and said he might do it.

About two months later I was in his area and he came up to me and thanked me for the conversation we had. He told me he did bring the picture to his work bench and it changed his life. He and his wife have never gotten *along better and he now has plenty of time for his three boys. Now when he goes hunting or fishing the boys go along. He told me he was finally having the relationship with his sons he always wanted.*

This small shift in where this man focused his attention about his job and why he worked at this company changed how he focused on his entire life.

chapter three

Truth

Webster's New Twentieth Century Dictionary, Unabridged Second Edition defines truth as, "that which is true; a fact; a reality; that which conforms to fact or reality; the real or true state of things." Truth as a concept seems very powerful in that it has directed and justified much of human behavior over the years. The problem I have with truth is I don't believe it exists.

Who and what we are as a person is the sum total of our God given qualities and abilities at birth or, if you prefer, our genetic predispositions plus our own personal experiences throughout our lives. These two components combine to make up the individuals we are every day. Every new experience and learning adds information; therefore, changing who we are and how we behave. I believe truth is just a judgment call dependent upon the person identifying truth and his or her current map of the world.

The collective knowledge of mankind is continuously expanding. We examine previous ideas, beliefs, and information and expand the things we have identified and believe to be accurate while we discard any beliefs which prove to be inaccurate. Many of the truths which directed mankind have been found inaccurate by the addition of new information and changing technologies. This causes us to alter our map of the world; therefore, affecting the judgment call identifying truth.

Some examples of this process of *changing truths* may be seen in the belief that the world was flat or that the earth was the center of the universe. Imagine yourself traveling back in time 100 years and describing your world today to your own ancestors. I am not sure where I would even start.

One belief which I have been thinking about lately is Newton's Law of Gravity. My entire life I have been told and believed that what goes up must always come down. If you jump out of a window ten stories high you will always go down and never go up. The law of gravity appears very basic to our world and as true as life itself.

Applying new technology in the '60's mankind has been able to expand the context of the Natural Laws of Our World through the ability to send space craft out of the gravitational forces of earth. An astronaut jumping out of the shuttle not only will not fall, he doesn't even know which way is down. He is still a human being and subject to other laws of nature, but Newton's Law of Gravity is not applicable in this context. Many truths are dependent upon the context of evaluation. Whenever we change or expand the context we also may change the truth or how that truth affects our lives.

I offer my position on truth because ironically the people who first begin the construction of our walls such as our family, friends, and schools have only our best interests motivating their actions. They are only attempting to guide us toward truth in hopes of improving our lives. The obvious problem is their truth and maps of the territory may or may not support us in our growth to becoming the person we choose. We must find our own truth and live by our standards and these walls can inhibit that process.

I have never been an astronaut and can only imagine the feelings of fear mixed with excitement and possibility that must be the experience of those getting aboard to travel into space. They are entering a new time and space where previous beliefs and understandings may not be applicable. Each of us enter a new time and place where previous beliefs and understandings may not be applicable whenever we break through our existing walls, search and find our own truth, and actively and consciously direct our own lives.

Please take a moment and think back to a belief which you really knew was true but as you progressed through life you learned new information which caused you to change that judgment. What impact did this new truth have on your behavior and understanding of your world?

Thoughts for consideration

If our truths are accurate, considering other possibilities will reinforce their accuracy.

The following is how I remember the fable about three blind men and the elephant.

Three blind men, having no experience with an elephant, meet one in the jungle.

The first blind man touches the elephant's tail and says, "I now know what an elephant is: It is like a piece of rope."

The second blind man touches the elephant's leg and says, "I now know what an elephant is: It is like the trunk of a tree."

The third blind man touches the elephant's side and says, "I now know what an elephant is: It is like a large boulder."

Each blind man returned home confident that he now knows what an elephant is.

Often people identify their truth very much as did the three blind men. Considering only part of an issue can leads us to believing in false truths.

Which of the three boys below is the tallest?

Apparently the third boy in line is taller than the other two boys.

Use a ruler or some other measuring device and you will discover that all three boys are the same height.

This picture is an optical illusion and depends upon your perspective in comparing one boy to the others and their relationship to the rest of the picture.

Your perspective can be very powerful when identifying truth; however, it can also be very misleading.

Have you ever decided not to follow your dream, not to get involved in a project, given up on something important to you, or just sold yourself short because of your perspective on your abilities and worth as a person compared to how you perceived the ability or worth of other people or the world you live in?

Is it possible your decision was based on faulty perspective?

Could you have underestimated your value or over estimated the ability and value of another person?

Is it possible that you have developed some limiting beliefs about yourself or your place in society that keeps you somewhat stuck where you are?

Could these beliefs be based on an inaccurate perspective possibly directed by other people's evaluation of your ability?

You should focus your attention on your own abilities because you are the person living your life. Comparing yourself to abilities others appear to possess may lead you to develop a false or limiting perspective about yourself. Any such comparisons may well be just as misleading as the picture of the three boys.

chapter four

Pause

Stimulus -> Pause -> Response

These three words identify the orderly process of how the human mind functions and interacts with its environment; thus, directing behavior. Stimulus can be external to yourself or it can be an internal motivation of a new thought. Response is our reaction to the stimulus. Pause is the space or time between the stimulus and the response. It can be an instant or an extended period.

Reality dictates *if you keep doing the same thing, in the same way, you will get the same results*. Let me ask you a question: Are you currently happy and satisfied with all the aspects of your life? If you are truly happy and satisfied please continue living exactly the same way because you are already getting your desired results. However, if some change is appropriate, I recommend you utilize *pause* which allows you to take control of your state of mind and the direction of your life.

One of the few elements in our lives over which I believe we have total control is our own integrity. Integrity is what we choose to do with the information we believe true. Unfortunately, we cannot control the accuracy of the information and we may make honest mistakes in responding to what we believe to be true. Sometimes moving from stimulus directly to response can compromise our integrity. Whenever we compromise our integrity we also compromise our self-respect.

Relative to our understanding of the concept of walls, our response has a tendency of being rote or favoring whatever previous patterns we have developed. I believe no event or stimulus has only one response and which ever response we choose excludes other options. When we get out of bed in the morning we chose not to stay in bed and every choice we make the rest of the day is a trade-off of options.

Obviously there are many aspects of your life when rote reaction to stimulus is the correct choice. An example is when you are driving a car and the traffic light turns red; you respond with the appropriate reaction of stepping on the brake. I wonder, in how many aspects of your life are you not getting your desired results, yet your rote patterned responding is directing you to doing the same things in the same way. Rather then proceeding directly from stimulus to response, the following three steps will allow a more productive and positive use of *pause.*

Gather the facts and information
Identify and evaluate the options
Choose your response

Gather the facts and information

Gathering the facts is not always an easy process. Our walls often limit our ability to be objective and see what is in front of our eyes. Gathering the facts which only support our existing perspective is not really gathering the facts. Many times it is helpful to consider the direct opposite of our first evaluation, or evaluate from another person's perspective.

Thirteen months ago my son Kevin was born. Watching him grow and make sense of his world I realized how differently from me he must see the world. He has not established strong preconceived beliefs or walls directing his interpretation of what he experiences. My wife and I laugh as we buy him what we feel are stimulating and fun toys because we know we will watch him have a happy experience with an old shoe he discovers in the corner, leaving his wonderful toys in the middle of the room.

Remember, the truth of our facts is only a judgment call. We must always be willing to challenge that call by seeking new information. Being childlike is being very curious and open to seeing what is there without a great number of preconceptions. Often new information is outside the walls of our current perception of the world.

Is this curve concave or convex? Gathering facts, similar to identifying truth, depends on your perspective.

Identify and Evaluate the Options

Our minds function by constantly asking and answering questions. Should I get up in the morning? Should I stay in bed this morning? Evaluating the information we gather is the same process. We ask and answer questions about the information. The effectiveness of our evaluation is directly linked to the quality of our questions. Whenever we feel out of control in evaluating the options we are usually asking the wrong questions or focusing on the wrong options. These wrong questions tend to be restrictive or limiting with a negative overtone. Notice the word *why* can be useful while seeking additional information, but it often receives very negative, defensive, and limiting responses.

For example:

Why did this happen to me?
Why can't he understand my position?
Why can't I quit smoking? lose weight?

Listen to the questions you are currently asking and be sure to use questions which require a positive, growth directed, and expanding response.

For example:

How can I use this event to grow and improve my future?
How can I help him understand my position?
What can I do to quit smoking? lose weight?
How will my life improve when I quit smoking? lose weight?
What can I learn from this experience?
What other options are available?

Asking better more expanding questions requires better more supportive answers which may lead us to new options currently outside our walls.

Presuppositions and assumptions can drastically effect our identification and understanding of the options and inhibit our ability to ask and answer the most effective questions. Many times I have heard the following question, while the questioner holds up a half of a glass of water: "Is this glass half-full or half-empty?" The answer half-empty identifies a person focusing with a negative outlook and conversely the half-full response identifies one with a positive representation of life.

The presupposition or assumption that the glass is either half-empty or half-full, with the answer indicating the person's attitude toward life, may not be accurate. My belief is additional questions are necessary before I have enough information and options to give my best answer. One question I feel appropriate is: Was the glass being filled or emptied? This question would accurately indicate if the glass was half-full or half-empty. Until then I have only half a glass of water.

The half-full or half-empty glass question illustrates two separate issues. The first is often the presuppositions or assumptions we are conditioned to accept or believe to be true (walls) modify our perception of reality and our ability to identify our options. The second issue is goal-setting. Knowing the direction we are going with our lives has a strong impact on our identification and evaluation of the options we have and assist us in making our best choices.

Choose your response

Choosing the response that best supports who you are and where you are going is not always as clear or simple as most of us prefer. One night, while eating dinner, my sister-in-law was sharing her concern about some choices she was evaluating at that time in her life. She questioned why each of us were not born with an instruction manual to guide us through the choices in our lives. I told her I believed we do have an instruction manual built inside and when we have to make a decision our instincts direct our behavior. Good choices just feel right. My wife added that sometimes you have to just be quiet and listen for the answers. Often the walls created by other people's expectations and opinions make it difficult to hear and follow our operating instructions.

One method of evaluation I have found very helpful is the Ben Franklin decision-making process. According to the story, Ben Franklin used the balance sheet approach whenever he had to make a difficult decision. Ben would draw a line down the middle of a sheet of paper and on one side list all the pros he could identify and on the other side all the cons. You can also make the headings: *What will happen if I do?* and *What will happen if I don't?* The process of writing out the Ben Franklin method allows us to eliminate some of the vagueness of the problem, more accurately and completely identify and evaluate the options, and make the best choice.

For example:

PROS	CONS
Write the book Walls	Not write the book Walls
I will enjoy the satisfaction and pride of achievement of sharing my world in hope of helping people improve their lives; thus, having a positive effect on the world.	I will continue to see the problems of the world as too big and overwhelming
I will have the knowledge I did something to positively effect the problems I see rather than just talking and complaining.	I will continue to ask the question, What can one man do? I will continue answering, One man can do nothing; therefore, just keep complaining and feeling like a victim.
I have offered some ideas for people to be more at choice in their lives with an attitude of abundance as opposed to being not at choice with an attitude of scarcity which seems so prevalent today.	

Pause is a simple word defined by Webster as a "short period of inaction" or "a temporary stop or rest." I wonder if you notice how many times each day you go from stimulus directly to response without stopping to take conscious advantage of *pause* to gather new information, evaluate new options, and make new and different choices. How would new and different choices positively affect your life?

[*PAUSE*]

It could be very interesting!

Thoughts for consideration

Are you aware of some of the patterns in your life?
Are you willing to search for new responses?

In the differences among people lies the greatest source of new ideas and beliefs which can lead us to developing new responses.

Most people prefer being in comfortable surroundings with people who share similar beliefs and views of the world. Have you ever noticed when people meet for the first time they ask questions which attempt to discover things they have in common and when they find some the conversation stays on the common items.

Many of the things we respond to are external events or other people's actions. One of my favorite stories is about Buddha and how he reacted to an aggressor.

Buddha

Buddha was an enlightened wise man, a religious philosopher and teacher who lived in India and was the founder of Buddhism. One day Buddha was teaching a group of people when a man came to the front of the group and shouted offensive and insulting statements at Buddha. Buddha listened for a short while and then softly asked the man, "May I ask you a question?" The man agreed and Buddha asked the following, "If you bring me a valuable present and I refuse to accept it, who does the present belong to?" The man thought and answered, "the present would still belong to me." Buddha agreed and asked another question, "When you bring to me insults and anger and I refuse to accept them, who do the insults and anger belong to?" The man thought for a moment and then turned away and left the group.

Being responsible for your own life includes being in control of your emotions. In order to effectively evaluate and explore options we must remain in control of our thinking process.

Sometimes other people enter our world with anger, criticism, insults, disrespect, and other such qualities which can offend us. Often they do not even recognize they are offending us because they are focused on their own world and we just happen to be there. This also happens when people have their expectations of what we should do or how we should live. When we allow them to enter our thinking process we give away our ability to make the best most supportive choices for ourselves.

Whenever you notice yourself allowing a person or event to invade your thinking process, think about Buddha and remember you do have control over how you react to external events. Ignoring the person and not even recognizing their existence or responding to what ever they have said may be the best way to deal with the situation. Nobody likes to be ignored and it is often a very disarming response.

What do you see in the picture below?

You may see three arrows, three home plates, or three houses on their side. Do you also see the two capital Ks?

What do you see in the picture below?

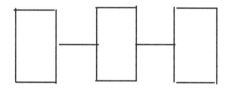

Very likely you see two capital Hs.

Why did you see the two Hs so quickly?
Did you gather new information from the first picture?
Did that information change where you focused your attention?

Gathering new information and developing a new strategy is essential in developing new responses.

chapter five

Enhancing Patterns

A powerful understanding is to realize the past events and choices in our lives are the building blocks for a better future. Ironically, the knowledge which directs our good choices often comes from the experience we gain from our bad choices.

Seemingly people tend to have behavior patterns which activate very rapidly, without conscious thought, going directly from stimulus to response with little or no attention to pause. The handicap this creates is, *if we continue doing the same things, in the same way, we will get the same results*; therefore, remaining captive within our walls.

I have had times in my life when I made bad choices and the results were totally unacceptable. My internal dialogue at that point went something like this: Boy am I dumb!, Why did I do that?, This is a fine mess I have gotten myself into this time!, and other similar statements and questions that only reinforce my own lack of ability and self-worth.

Looking back, I now realize I didn't always make bad choices but often I made no conscious choice at all. I simply allowed outside stimulus to activate nonsupportive behavior patterns which led to nonsupportive results. I then reinforced these patterns by focusing on the results with negative and restrictive questions and statements. Now whenever I find myself getting unacceptable results I ask better questions like **What could I have done differently?** or **What might have been a better choice?** These questions don't change the unacceptable results I have already realized, but in the future whenever a similar situation arises, I can notice the behavior pattern starting, interrupt the pattern, and shift to alternative choices.

This technique of evaluation doesn't work only for today's unacceptable results. I was able to recall many other events in my life and identify nonsupportive patterns and examine different choices which may have led to far better results. This process allows me to maximize my experience of all previous events by evaluating different options that were available. This doesn't change the past but develops greater flexibility in creating my future. My definition of unacceptable results is anything in your life that is in conflict with or doesn't support the image of who you are and who you want to become.

I would like to share a very personal experience and how the use of *pause* has expanded my personal options and greatly enhanced my life. My father died over twenty years ago and as I remember what I knew of his life, I believe he was a good man and I believe he loved me. However, he did not seem satisfied with his life and seemed to have a lot of internal frustration and anger. Unfortunately his method of relating to and directing me was very negative and we never enjoyed a close relationship. Thinking back as far as I can remember into my childhood, he would smack me on the back of my head (not to hurt me but to get my attention) and say in an angry disgusted tone of voice, with an angry ugly look on his face, "You are the G. D. stupidest little S.O.B. I have ever seen! You can't be my son, there must be some mistake!" After a while just a few angry words or the angry ugly glare conveyed that same message very clearly.

You can probably imagine some of the nonsupportive patterns I developed, yet even as a small boy I somehow never totally accepted his interpretation and evaluation of my value as a person. I did, however, develop the pattern of never really applying myself to any specific goal. Somehow I believed if I never really committed myself, then I could never actually fail, and my father could never be right in his view of my worth. I remember failing the fourth grade, yet inside I knew I could do the work if I wanted, but I chose not to perform. This pattern obviously was not supportive.

Fortunately for me, I was able to float through life doing all right with whatever came my way and even completed college while on a football scholarship. When I was twenty-two years old, I was evaluating some current results in my life that had not gone my way. I suddenly realized, as if a light went on, I had never really focused on any goal in my life.

By identifying my restrictive pattern of floating through life without goals, I was able to go back to the beginning stimulus and re-evaluate the structure and accuracy of this pattern. I didn't go back as a child and re-experience the event. I went back as the adult I had become, somewhat like watching a movie about a boy and his father. This experience allowed me to identify, evaluate, and understand a very restrictive pattern that short-circuited and limited many of the options and choices that directed my life.

I am now forty-six years old and I must confess I still notice the old patterns attempting to engage and direct my behavior. Seemingly old patterns will try to shift me directly from stimulus to old responses the rest of my life. Noticing the process and consciously using *pause* to choose my response are the tools I use to overcome old patterns and direct my life.

The following is a method or technique for evaluating a past event which may have developed into a nonsupportive pattern. Please understand you do not want to relive the event or fully associate with the feelings and emotions but disassociate from the event and treat it as a process of evaluation. Imagine you are watching a movie and you are the director. It is your movie and you can direct it any way you choose. As an example of the process I have shared my own experience after each step.

STEP 1
Identify a result or behavior which does not support who you are or who you want to become.

I have considered writing this book for a long time, yet never got started.

66

STEP 2

These patterns have a sequence and structure which tend to engage with a trigger event. Think back through the series of events just before this result or behavior you have identified. This will identify the pattern of the behavior and you want to locate the trigger or event which started the sequence.

The following is my internal thought sequence for the result of *not starting*:

#1 *Finding more important things to do while saying: I will start later.*

#2 *Focusing on and internally experiencing feelings of fear of rejection.*

#3 *Asking myself nonsupportive questions: What do I know? Who cares what I have to share?*

#4 *Considering limiting beliefs. I can't write well. People don't really want to change. I am too busy to take the time to write a book.*

#5 *I have to actually write the book and display my inner thoughts for evaluation. If the book is not successful my father will be right in his opinion of my abilities and worth.*

#6 *The **TRIGGER**. I have to totally commit myself to a goal. When my committing to a goal is appropriate it engages the pattern leading to not getting started.*

STEP 3

You are directing this evaluation process so think back to right before the trigger or stimulus which started the pattern. Consider your options from this view point knowing the result you don't want. What better choices or meaning to the event can you construct and engage when the trigger or stimulus occurs?

When committing myself to a goal I can challenge myself to grow and develop and use all of my abilities. Not committing makes me a loser in my own mind because I would be quitting on myself. That would really make my father right!

STEP 4
Imagine how the movie now plays or how these new choices and behavior will create a better more supportive result.

Having committed to write this book I am researching, gathering information, and developing abilities which were previously outside my walls. I am having fun and I am excited about this new adventure.

STEP 5
Look into the future, beyond the present time, and decide if these new choices take you where you want to go with your life.

I envision myself very satisfied because I have written this book. I truly believe the information I am sharing will have a positive influence on some people, helping them improve their lives. This belief supplies some purpose and meaning to my life.

This technique for evaluating patterns and past events allows us to maximize and take advantage of our experiences and expand many of our future options. It also makes us more aware of the patterns and walls in our lives, which gives us more conscious control of our choices and behavior in the future.

Reflecting on my relationship with my father, I now understand I have the power to go back to things in my life which may have caused me to establish nonsupportive patterns or negative self-image and re-evaluate those experiences. I know I cannot change the events that happened in my past, but I do have the ability to let go of any negative emotions like anger, hate, or revenge, which motivate behavior patterns that continue to limit my choices and options and short-circuit my quest to become who and what I choose.

Thoughts for consideration

*The first step in enhancing patterns is to identify them and
realize you have control of them. Noticing the pattern
allows you to call "Time Out!", explore different options,
and direct your thinking and behavior in a more supportive
direction.*

What are some of your restrictive patterns?
When do they engage?
What triggers them engaging?
What may be a more supportive behavior?
Do you have power over these patterns?

*The relationship I had with my father is an example of my
letting another person enter my thinking process and direct
my self-image and my emotional state. This developed a
very restrictive pattern which had a tremendous impact on
my life.*

*Morris Massey identified the imprint stage of development
as birth thru age seven. When we are young we have little
defense against this type of invasion because we have very
limited life experience. When a loved one invades our
thinking with their limiting beliefs it is very hard to resist
their influence because we trust them. Fortunately, like all
patterns, once we identify them we can identify and choose
different patterns.*

Our past is our memories of an event from the perspective of who we were at that time. Talk with a family member or friend about things that you experienced together in the past. Notice any differences between your memories and theirs. No two people see or remember things exactly the same way. We are not the same person we were in the past because we have more experience at living and being ourselves which affects how we evaluate events.

A few years ago I attended a seminar and the following idea was offered: "Life is a live performance, there are no dress rehearsals." At the time I liked the thought and I believe we need to live in the present; however, I do think we can have dress rehearsals. When we use our thoughts and imagination we can visualize our future and we actually practice what and how we will perform. This method of evaluating our past and identifying additional choices to engage if similar events occur in the future is living in the present and rehearsing for the future.

Each day notice other people's situations and how they choose to respond. Television, movies, books, newspapers, and magazines offer the opportunity to evaluate the choices people made and consider what other choices were available. We can learn from other people's experience just as well as our own. This practice of exploring and evaluating various responses will assist us in making the best choices if similar events occur in our lives.

When we evaluate past events it is important to understand what we learned from those events. We do have the power to change by learning from our experience and altering our behavior.

What keeps us stuck with past events is the emotions we assigned to the event. Emotions like anger, fear, hate, revenge, shame, feeling inferior, or other negative emotions keep the events alive and part of our present. Often these events were when other people did cruel or abusive things to us. When we maintain the emotions of the event we are allowing that person or event to continue to negatively affect our life.

Remember they are our memories. We can keep the things we learned and let the emotions go. Yesterday is gone, unless we choose to bring the emotions of yesterday's events into our today.

Consider the 6 P words in the following sentence.
Planning, Preparation & Practice Prevent Poor Performance.

> Learn from the mistakes of others--
> you can never live long enough
> to make them all yourself.
> Anonymous

chapter six

Values

Les Miserables is my favorite play and the most powerful production I have ever experienced. During one scene, Jean Valjean, one of the main characters, an ex-convict and parole breaker, has taken a new identity and becomes the mayor of the town. Javert, a policeman who has been tracking Jean Valjean for years, meets with the mayor. Javert notices something familiar about Valjean, but explains he has come to town because they have just captured the parole breaker, number 24601, Jean Valjean, and will be taking him back to prison where he belongs.

This turn of events will allow the real Jean Valjean to continue his new life as Mayor of the town, but he will have to let an innocent man go to prison in his place. Jean Valjean asks himself the question, "Who am I?" The answer to this question, evaluating his core values which make him the person he is, will direct his behavior and drastically affect the direction of the rest of his life. This mental evaluation leads him to his final choice, "If I speak out, I am condemned. If I stay silent, I am damned." Jean Valjean makes his decision consistent with his own core values and goes to the courthouse identifying himself as the real Jean Valjean. This allows the innocent man to go free. Jean Valjean escapes leaving everything behind as he goes on to the next stage of his life.

Who am I? is a very powerful question because your core values direct and motivate all of your behavior. Additionally your core values evaluate the outcome of all your behaviors. These core values are the essence of who you are, yet most people cannot readily and accurately list their top ten most important values and consciously understand the impact they have on their lives. Many people believe core values are imprinted on us before we are seven years old. This would indicate we didn't choose our core values but had them conditioned for us while we were small children.

Sociologist Morris Massey's research on the creation of values identifies three developmental periods in the creation of core values: Imprint Period, birth to age seven; Modeling Period, age eight thru age thirteen; and the Socialization Period, from age fourteen thru twenty-one.

What are values? This question is hard to accurately answer because values tend to be somewhat vague and the words are open to individual interpretation. Many times values are expressed in what linguists term nominalizations, that is action words or predicates used as nouns.

Example of nominalizations:

noun	verb or predicate
freedom	free
satisfaction	satisfy
contribution	contribute

I believe values are the aspects of our lives which validate the meaning and purpose of our existence, or more simply, values are whatever is important to us as people.

A person's character is the manifestation of their core values over a lifetime. I have understood the importance of core values for a long time and if asked if I could write and prioritize my top 10 values I would confidently answer **YES**! A few months ago I decided to write out my top 10 values and much to my surprise I really wasn't able to complete the list. Actually it took me several weeks of playing with the project before I finally identified my top 10 values. The experience has had a profound effect on my ability to answer the question, Who am I? I now have a clearer understanding of what motivated my behavior in many past events in my life and I feel better prepared to make conscious choices in the future.

Considering the concept of walls, we first have to catch ourselves inside our walls and use the element of *pause* to identify and evaluate our choices. Values are the operating instructions which will direct the evaluation of our options. Conscious awareness and understanding of our values provide us with the knowledge to make the best choices supporting behavior consistent with who we are.

Many people I have met over the years who were experiencing difficulty in their lives, especially in the areas of self-direction and self-responsibility, seemed to share a similar problem. Their behavior was in conflict with their values. This internal conflict produced negative results often affecting self-image. These conflicts can be minor or they can overwhelm us, preventing us from identifying any options, thus trapping us within our walls.

Values are also the foundation of our beliefs and rules which govern our behavior on a more conscious level of awareness. Beliefs are those ideas which identify what we consider to be true in our world and they establish and direct the rules we apply to our behavior. The reality of beliefs is that they often change with the addition of new information or when evaluated in a different context. Rules are the most conscious directors of our behavior; however, when they are externally created they often become the building blocks of our walls.

A few months ago I was talking with a high school friend about values and he said he believed his values have changed quite a lot over the years. As we discussed the changes it became evident that his beliefs and rules had changed with the addition of new information and the experience of maturing, becoming a husband and a father, and, in general, just growing through his life; however, his core values had not changed at all. He still uses the same core values to evaluate his options. The options changed because he was evaluating new information from the perspective of who he is today. The beliefs and rules also changed consistent with this new evaluation. Ending the conversation we both agreed that today we basically use the same values that we used earlier in our lives to direct our behavior and evaluate our choices.

Last week I was talking with an old college teammate about values and as you can probably guess, I asked if he could identify his top 10 core values. He thought for a short period and then told me that about six years ago he became a Christian and the beliefs of Christianity definitely added a great deal of value to his life. He then identified his belief that the Ten Commandments were his top values.

I believe the Ten Commandments are wonderful rules to govern your behavior in life, but I do not think they are values. Your true core life values motivate and direct you to believe in the Ten Commandments and support you in applying them in directing your behavior.

What are your core values? Can you write them out and understand how they direct your behavior? If you answer *yes*, then do it again now to reinforce this powerful knowledge. If you are like I was, answering confidently *YES*! and moving along, but never actually writing out your top 10 values, I believe the exercise will be worth the effort and will supply you with new and interesting information about yourself.

Make a list of your values and then go back prioritizing them in their order of importance. My personal experience and observations of others indicate the top two, three, or four values seem somewhat obvious and easy to identify. The commitment to identify ten or twelve values directs you to a much deeper, profound understanding of who you are. This second level of values often reveals the most interesting new information.

The question you want to answer to identify your values is: *What is most important to me about life? about work? about play? about my relationships?* Having created your list of 10 or 12 core values which accurately reflect your understanding of what is really important in your life, go back and put the values in their order of importance using the same question: *What is most important to me in my life? What is next most important to me in my life?* Sometimes the choices become difficult to distinguish. In these cases consider which you would choose if you could only pick one. I believe there are times and events that may cause a shift in the order of importance, so don't get too bogged down on values which are so close in your hierarchy. This usually isn't a problem for the top three or four, but seems to increase as you get further down your list.

The purpose of this exercise is to consciously understand yourself and more accurately answer the question, **Who am I?** You will become aware of any conflicts among your values or conflicts among your values, beliefs, and rules. Eliminating these internal conflicts will motivate and direct more supportive behavior, allowing you to break through the walls and consciously choose your path for your life.

The following is my list of values which will give you additional insight into who I am and the world according to Callahan. I have also supplied a list of some values which may help you in identifying your own. There are no right or wrong values in this exercise. Remember describing values with words can appear vague and open to interpretation; therefore, be certain you clearly understand

what your values are and what they mean to you and write
them as specifically as you can.

Jim Callahan's values hierarchy:

> Balance-oneness-peace of mind
> Self-respect
> Integrity
> Meaning and purpose
> Love
> Contribution
> Enthusiasm
> Compassion
> Health
> Growth-learning

This list may help you in considering your values.

achievement	goodwill	power
adventure	gratefulness	purpose
attractiveness	growth	recognition
balance	health	respect
beauty	helpfulness	reward
boldness	honesty	security
challenge	humor	self-respect
cheerfulness	individuality	spirituality
cleverness	integrity	stability
confidence	intelligence	strength
contribution	intimacy	success
consideration	joy	supportiveness
comfort	justice	tenderness
compassion	kindness	togetherness
creativity	knowledge	understanding
enthusiasm	learning	uniqueness
excitement	love	vision
family	meaning	vitality
fairness	money	warmth
fitness	organization	wealth
flexibility	outrageousness	wisdom
forgiveness	passion	wonderment
freedom	peace of mind	
friends	persistence	
fun	positiveness	

Thoughts for consideration

Attending the play <u>Les Miserables</u> and evaluating the choices of Jean Valjean directed me to identify my core values. This is an example of enhancing patterns by watching other people, which we discussed in the previous chapter.

Do you know what your core values are and how they direct your choices?

Do you believe your values direct your choices?

Can you answer the questions, Who am I? What does my life stand for?

Could consciously knowing and focusing on your core values help you answer these questions?

Would evaluating your choices in consideration of your values direct a better evaluation?

Did you decide on your values because they represent how you choose to live your life or were they imprinted on you at an early age?

Are they your values or the values of your society?

Please imagine yourself in front of a group of the significant people in your life such as your family, close friends, religious leaders, and personal and professional peers. Now imagine turning and saying to the group: "If more people in this world live and conduct their lives as I do, the world would be a better place."

How would you feel saying this to the group?

Many people feel uncomfortable saying this sentence to anyone and some feel it is a very egoistical statement. Actually, the statement is asking you to identify how you live and conduct your life compared to how you believe people should live. This exercise may help you discover areas in your life where you are living in conflict with your values and beliefs about how people should live.

What are some of your beliefs?
For example:
> *I believe people are good or bad, kind or violent, equal or not equal.*

How do your beliefs direct your reality?
How do they affect your behavior?

What are some of your rules?
For example:
> *If I am good to people, they will be good in return.*
> *If I work hard I will succeed.*
> *Get the other guy before he gets you.*
> *Look out for yourself because nobody else will.*

How do your rules direct your reality?
How do they affect your behavior?

Do your beliefs and rules expand or restrict your thinking and your choices?

What are your rules for:
   Love?
   Respect?
   How others should treat you?
   How you should treat others?
   Fairness?
   Equality?

Do you make as much effort to identify and comply with other people's rules as you want them to identify and comply with your rules?

What happens when you violate another person's rules?
Do you think it might lead to conflict?
What if you don't know what rule you violated? Does it eliminate the conflict?
How do you react when somebody violates one of your rules?
Does it matter if they don't know your rules?

Have your values changed during your life?
How about your beliefs and rules?
What caused or motivated these changes?
Do you have the ability to make conscious changes in your values, beliefs, and rules?
Imagine how these changes will affect your life.

The value of freedom

The following is a discussion I had with a group of about 25 inmates at the Graterford Correctional Institution in Pennsylvania. These inmates participate in the organization "People Against Recidivism" which is a program for inmates established and run by inmates. We discussed values and the value of freedom.

I asked if freedom would be high on their list of values. They all agreed that freedom would be first or no less than second. Later they identified freedom would be number one or two for any inmate anywhere in the world.

I asked, What does the word freedom mean to you? They responded by telling me that at first they believed freedom was being out of prison, but decided that freedom had a much deeper meaning. They agreed freedom was the ability to make decisions in their lives, to identify choices, and to choose the one they believed correct. It seems ironic that they had to lose their freedom to understand what freedom really means to them.

I asked how many people they know on the outside who give their freedom away every day to drugs, alcohol, peer pressure, and limiting beliefs about what is possible. They told me it is more the rule than the exception where they lived.

Next we discussed: If freedom is number one or two on inmate's value chart while in prison, what causes so many to fall back to the same old pattern when they get out, which leads them back to prison? The inmates understand that old patterns are hard to break and they realize they stop focusing their attention on the value of freedom once they are out of prison.

This discussion helped these men understand the importance of their core values and they understood the value of focusing on them to help direct their life. We discussed anchoring the sights, sounds, and feelings of the value of freedom to deep breathing. (see Thoughts for consideration in chapter thirteen, "Emotional State Control") This gave them a tool to practice and use as a pattern interrupt when they noticed themselves starting to run an old pattern. They can take a deep breath and call back their experience of the value of freedom. This breaks the pattern and allows them to make better choices.

What some people consider values are actually the means of attaining the core value. e.g. Many people list "Family" as a value. "Family" is a means value which is how you get to ends values like love, commitment, belonging, intimacy, meaning, and purpose. This distinction does not eliminate "Family" from your values list. It allows for a clearer understanding of the value.

There are also moving-toward values and moving-away from values. Often moving-toward values have a reciprocal away from value. I believe when we focus on positive moving-toward values, that is what expands in our lives. (e.g. moving-toward wealth--moving-away from poverty)

My Values

Brainstorm and write in the first column anything you think is a value in your life. These are randomly written with no order of importance.

In column two write your values in the order of importance and mark each with a (M) for means value or an (E) for ends value. My belief is you should list the moving-toward values as your core values and be aware of the moving-away from values; however, this is your values list so it should represent your values and what is most important to you.

Random Values   *(M/E) My Values*

1 _____
2 _____
3 _____
4 _____
5 _____
6 _____
7 _____
8 _____
9 _____
10_____
11_____
12_____
13_____
14_____
15_____

chapter seven

Joe the Bartender

Joe the Bartender could be the most effective counselor and confidant in your city or town. Joe spends much of his day listening to people pour out their troubles and many leave feeling much better about their problems. Have you ever shared your problems with another person, possibly your hairdresser, your barber, or a bartender and during the conversation found the answers to your own questions?

Our minds receive and store a great deal of information at the subconscious level. This raw data is collected through our five senses on a continuous basis and is not sorted or classified by conscious standards. The process of transferring this raw data or information stored in the subconscious mind to the conscious level is to assign internal representations and words to the data.

The representations people assign to this raw data is usually in the form of three representational preferences: visual, auditory, or kinesthetic. There are two other representational systems: olfactory (smell) and gustatory (taste), yet these don't appear very often in bringing raw data to the conscious level. Visual people tend to create pictures in their minds, auditory people hear sounds, and kinesthetic people experience feelings. No one is limited to only one category but we do have preferences of one representational system over the others.

Joe the Bartender's success is based on the reality that people communicate using words and expressions. In order for people to share their problems with Joe they have to convert the raw data into language. Step one is to draw the appropriate information from the raw data pool at the subconscious level and get a clear representation at the conscious level. Step two is to convert these representations, the pictures, sounds, and feelings into words to communicate the problems to Joe.

I believe many of the problems or difficulties we deal with are often in that vague area, just below our conscious level. We are aware of their existence and they may cause us discomfort and pain, but we don't consciously and clearly understand the elements of their composition. This process of sharing with others using language directs us to clarify the issues and in the process we often discover the answers to our own questions. Whenever the problem is not clear enough at the conscious level to share with another person it is also not clear enough to solve. We usually have the answers to our own questions but both the questions and the answers are in that vague pool of subconscious knowledge just below our conscious awareness.

One method of identifying and addressing your own problems is to find Joe the Bartender. The less the person you choose to talk with knows about you and your life, the more effective the process. When we talk with friends who really know us, we tend to assume they understand our situation and comprehend what we are saying. Talking with a stranger or someone who doesn't know us very well directs us toward a clearer focus on the vague issues as we clarify and choose the words to identify and explain our problems.

Two years ago I started keeping a journal which I write in at least a few times a week. I discovered this a great vehicle to track and consciously understand many things happening in my life. I find it very interesting to go back and read where I was and what I was thinking over the past two years. This journal also provides a vehicle to identify any changes in my beliefs, rules, or the direction of my life.

I always write as if I am sharing my problems with another or leaving a legacy of who I am for those who follow. Keeping my journal allows me to convert much of the raw data collected each day into language. This verbalization of my experiences assists my conscious understanding and appreciation of every day.

Anybody not choosing to keep ongoing journals can use this writing process to address any individual problem. Writing out your problems in the privacy of your own world with the intention of converting the vague issues into language can clarify issues and answers. Remember to write as if you are explaining the problem or situation to someone you don't know.

Another format to write out your problems is the Ben Franklin balance sheet method of making decisions which we discussed back in the chapter on *Pause*.

If you are not comfortable discussing your problems with other people and prefer not to write out your questions and answers, another very effective option is the man or woman in the mirror. Often I go to the bathroom, close the door, look directly into my own eyes, and talk out loud about whatever is bothering me. At first I really felt uncomfortable and foolish, but much to my surprise, I soon began feeling very comfortable and secure with the mirror person's knowledge. I now understand the only person who can be totally supportive, compassionate, and understanding of my map of the territory is the person looking back from the mirror.

Whatever vehicle you choose to assist communication between the conscious level of thinking and the vague pool of information at the subconscious level will assist you in clearly identifying the issues and options in your life. Clear accurate thinking about our life depends upon our ability to create clear representations from the vague data at the subconscious level and to convert them into words and language at the conscious level. Often we tend to use vague words and phrases filled with incorrect generalizations and presumptions which lead to fuzzy and inaccurate conscious understanding. The following will identify some of the more common vague language patterns and some questions you can ask yourself or other people to clarify and understand the real issues.

The first pattern, universal qualifiers, occur when we use words such as all, every, never, always, nobody, and everybody. This pattern takes one event or one person and groups it with the entire universe of that event or person. Using universal qualifiers doesn't specify the event or person causing the problem. The entire universe of a person or event is too big or overwhelming to address; therefore, we cannot identify any acceptable options. When we break this pattern we establish a more defined understanding of the situation, allowing us to pursue more supportive behavior.

For example:

> Things *never* go my way.
> I *always* come up short.
> *Everybody* is against me.
> *Nobody* likes me.

To break this pattern ask the universal qualifier as a question, or repeat the statement as a question:

> *Never*?
> *Always*?
> *Everybody*?
> Things *never* go your way?
> *Everybody* is against you?

Another question to break this pattern is:

> **Can you think of a time when** *things went your way?*, *You didn't come up short?*, or *Somebody did like you?*

The second pattern is vague representation and identification of nouns (people, places, and things) and verbs (the action or events taking place). The questions to break these patterns are: *Who or what specifically? How specifically?* These questions will draw out more specific information allowing a more accurate identification of the issues. Remember, it is very hard to solve a vague problem.

For example:

Statement:	Things never go my way.
Question:	*What things specifically* never go your way?
	How specifically don't things go your way?

Statement:	I always come up short.
Question:	*How specifically* do you come up short?
	What specifically are you short of?

Statement:	Everybody is against me.
Question:	*Who specifically* is against you?
	How specifically are they against you?

The third pattern is using words which suggest your behavior is controlled externally. This gives the responsibility for your behavior to a source outside of yourself that is usually not identified. Some words that identify the use of this pattern are: should, shouldn't, must, can't, have to, and need to. Some questions to break these patterns are: *What would happen if I did? What would happen if I didn't? What prevents or stops you?* Breaking the patterns which create a vague conscious understanding about who is in charge of our life allows us to choose and actively direct our own behavior and our lives.

For example:

Statement: I can't do that.
Question: *What would happen if you did? What prevents or stops you* from doing it?

Statement: I should work harder.
Question: *What would happen if you did? What will happen if you don't? What prevents or stops you* from working harder?

The fourth pattern deletes or limits the options in our world by vague comparison with an unidentified entity. Some words that indicate the use of this pattern are: too much, too many, good, better, best, and too expensive. The questions to break these patterns are: *Compared to what? Compared to who?* Breaking these patterns allows us to retrieve the options which were lost or limited due to comparison with vague and unspecified information.

For example:

Statement:	That class is too much work.
Question:	***Compared to what?***
	Compared to what other classes?

| Statement: | That person is the best. |
| Question: | The best ***compared to whom?*** |

All of these language patterns represent deletions, distortions, and generalizations of the information which inhibit a clear concise retrieval and interpretation of the data stored at the subconscious level. Breaking these language patterns will help you establish a clear and accurate understanding of whatever is troubling you and allow you to clearly share your problems with Joe the Bartender and yourself.

Let me ask you a question about your discussion with Joe the Bartender. Joe looks straight into your eyes and says, "I think I understand your problem but it seems to indicate a larger issue." Could he be right? What can you do next?

Possibly you have gotten stuck on one issue that is too specific and doesn't represent the entire situation. You need to expand the focus of your questions to identify the larger issues. Focusing on issues that are too specific can limit your ability to see the bigger picture. Sometimes we cannot see the forest because we are looking at the trees. Ask yourself: ***What can this issue be an example of? What could this identify?*** These questions will lead you to the larger issues and may open entirely new windows of opportunity.

Thoughts for consideration

We already have the answers to most of our own questions. All we have to do is bring them to our conscious level and choose the best ones.

Identifying and developing your own answers is more effective than having someone else tell you what they think is right. Other people can give us ideas to think about, but we must identify our own answers and be responsible for our own lives.

Keeping a journal is an effective method of talking with Joe the Bartender. As we search for the words to write in our journal we clarify many of our daily experiences. The journal is also a place for us to examine our own language patterns and improve our ability to identify and clearly express our thoughts.

If your life is worth living, it is worth keeping a record of who you are and how you saw your world at various times. Have you ever wondered about the people in your family that came before you? What do you really know about your mother and father and how they grew in their thinking as they lived their lives? How about your grandparents or great grandparents? Your journal is a vehicle to leave your legacy for those who follow you through this journey from birth to death.

Do you have the ability to discover your own answers?
Do you feel your life is worth recording and leaving for those who follow you? If not, do you want it to be?
What would you do differently with your life if you were leaving your journal for the people you loved like your children and grandchildren?
Could they learn from your good decisions? Could they learn from your mistakes?

The words we use and hear in our society can become overwhelming and limit our belief that we can do anything about the issues they describe. Consider words and phrases like: racism, violence, poverty, corrupt government, corrupt politicians, and second class education. Here is one I like: a lost generation. How do you lose a generation? Is it like losing your car keys? If you lost your car keys wouldn't you look for them and when you found them, pick them up?

When we improve our ability to clearly and accurately identify thoughts for ourselves and communicate our ideas to others we improve the quality of our life.

Cues for identifying representational preferences

Communication is one person sending a thought and another person receiving it. As the sender we have the ability to observe cues and tailor our message to the representational system of the receiver. To effectively communicate we have the responsibility of sending our message in the best format for the receiver to understand.

When we think about something, we bring data gathered and stored at the subconscious level to the conscious level. This process requires us to assign representations to the raw data. We all create these representations using our five senses internally and most people have a preferred system.

Visual people create pictures in their minds.
Auditory people hear sounds.
Kinesthetic people experience feelings.

Word choice
The words a person chooses are observable cues we can use to identify their preferred system.

For example:
Visual match, "I see what you mean."
Auditory match, "I hear what you are saying."
Kinesthetic match, " I grasp what you mean."

The following are some sample words and phrases:

Visual: see, look, imagine, watch, focus, picture, show, I see what you mean, you will look back at this and laugh, imagine that, watch your step, the future looks bright, we see eye to eye, beyond a shadow of a doubt, it appears to me

Auditory: hear, say, listen, noisy, loud, quiet, shout, scream, I hear what you are saying, listen to me, living in harmony, music to my ears, rings a bell, in a manner of speaking, loud and clear, things are beginning to click

Kinesthetic: feel, touch, warm, rough, smooth, heavy, firm, I grasp what you mean, I will get in touch with you, a warm-hearted man, I feel it in my bones, hold on a second, scratch the surface, a cool customer, I can't put my finger on it, a ticklish situation

Listen to the words the person uses and how they describe their experiences. When you identify a person's preferred system, you can construct your communication consistent with their system and communicate more effectively. You may find this difficult at first because you have your own representational system. As you play with the process you will increase your ability to effectively communicate.

Eye Movements

Eye movements are an effective behavioral indicator of a person's internal process. They are consistent and easy to detect. Neurological studies have shown that eye movement both laterally and vertically seems to be associated with activating different parts of the brain. They are called eye accessing cues because they are the visual cues that let us know how people are accessing information. There is some innate neurological connection between eye movements and representational systems. Unlike the person's descriptive word choice, which is usually constructed at a conscious level, eye accessing cues identify much of the process constructed out of a person's awareness.

The following eye movement patterns hold true for normally organized right-handed people. There may be some variations for left-handed people due to their difference in internal organization.

<u>Visual</u>: When people access pictures or visions their eyes look up. Up and to the right when creating new pictures and up and to the left when remembering pictures.

<u>Auditory:</u> When people access sounds their eyes remain in the level line from ear to ear. They look toward the right ear when creating a sound and to the left ear when remembering a sound.

<u>Kinesthetic:</u> When people access feelings they look down and to the right.

<u>Internal Dialogue</u>: When people are having a internal conversation they look down and to the left.

Practice observing the eye accessing cues and listening for descriptive words. The more accurately you identify someone's representation preference, the more effectively you can communicate with them.

To practice observing these cues find someone to work with and ask the following questions while noticing their eye movements. For left handed people ask the questions and notice their patterns, which may be the same or reversed.

Visual constructed;
Can you imagine a purple triangle inside a red square?
How will you look in twenty years?

Visual remembered;
What color is your front door?
Which of your friends has the longest hair?

Auditory constructed;
What would your voice sound like underwater?
How would your favorite tune sound at double speed?

Auditory remembered;
Which door slams loudest in your house?
Can you hear your favorite piece of music in your mind?
What is the sound of a telephone busy signal?

Kinesthetic (feelings):
How do you feel after a good meal?
What does it feel like to put on wet socks?
How do you feel when someone puts you down?

Internal dialogue;
What do you say to yourself when things go wrong?
When you talk to yourself, where does the sound come from?

These illustrations show eye movements patterns as they appear when observing a normally organized right-handed person.

Visual - Constructed Images

(Building An Image)

Visual - Recalled Images

(Remembering An Image)

Auditory - Constructing Words

(Building A Dialogue)

Auditory - Remembering Words

(Remembering A Dialogue)

Kinesthetic

(Internal & External Feeling)

Auditory - Internal Dialogue

(Carrying On An Internal Conversation)

chapter eight

Language

Let's consider language as a linking together of words which represent at a conscious level certain information we retrieve from our subconscious data pool. Language is how we consciously evaluate ideas and also how we share our thoughts with other people. Remember that the mind functions by consistently asking and answering questions. Words are only metaphors or symbols of sensory information we have collected. We must be aware that the words we choose to represent our interpretation of some data may have different meanings to other people and can even change in our internal dialogue depending on the context of our evaluation.

A good example of this varying representation of the same word is to consider the word *dog*, which seems a rather simple and common word. If you ask a thousand people the question: What is your representation of the word **dog**? you may get a thousand different answers.

Some people will internally see a dog; some will see a German shepherd, some a sheepdog, some a cocker spaniel, usually depending upon the dogs in their lives. Other people will hear a dog, possibly a dog growling, or a big or a small dog barking. Still others will have some internal feelings such as fear or affection as they interpret the word dog. Understanding how a thousand people could each have a different internal representation of the word dog, we can recognize the potential different representations for words like love, fear, hate, satisfaction, fairness, truth, and respect.

Language and words are very interesting because the words we choose to express our maps of the world indicate how we create our reality and often identify our walls. Every word we use is chosen at either a conscious or subconscious level, yet how often do we consciously hear and evaluate the words we have chosen?

I recently attended a Photo Reading program to learn a method of accelerated reading. During the lunch break a fellow attendee asked me if I was aware how often I used the word *trying* during my discussions with the trainer. I really wasn't even aware at a conscious level that I used the word *trying*.

This fellow attendee explained the word *trying* is a key signal word which identifies a negative expectation or a strong possibility of noncompletion. In my case, it identified my expectation that Photo Reading wasn't going to be effective for me. I was apprehensive about the program and questioned the process of Photo Reading. After our conversation I found myself focusing on the process rather then on my negative concerns. I noticed myself using the word *trying* and each time it entered my mind it exploded into my conscious awareness and I was able to adjust my focus toward the program and get outside my walls of negative expectations. This simple understanding allowed me to focus on the positive value of the Photo Reading program.

Before choosing to use the word *try* or *trying* you first have to create an internal representation of your inability to succeed or complete whatever you are discussing or considering. I had strong doubts about the possibility of Photo Reading; therefore, the signal word *trying* consistently appeared. If I had believed in Photo Reading or had no negative expectations, I would have used more positive words which would have indicated my openness to accept the process. I might say "I am learning the process of Photo Reading" instead of "I am *trying* to learn Photo Reading."

Consciously listen to your own words and notice yourself using the word *try* or *trying*. This exercise may uncover many things that currently consume much of your time and energy. It will also allow you to focus your attention on the things which you truly believe possible and beneficial.

Notice the relationship between satisfaction and expectation. I wonder how often we are not satisfied with the outcome of things in our lives and upon further evaluation we realized we obtained the exact results we really expected. Listen for the word *trying*.

Two additional words I find very fascinating and powerful are the words *but* and *why*. Linguistically the use of the word *but* negates the value or truth of whatever was just stated. When we enter this stage of communication, after the word *but*, we tend to feel the need to verify and prove our point. We now have conflict rather than expansion and growth of ideas.

Consider the following example:
> Person A says: *"It's a nice day."*
> Person B responds: *"Yes **but** it's supposed to rain."*
> Person A now feels challenged and needs to validate their statement about the nice day.

This example may seem very simple **but** have you ever had a similar experience while talking and sharing your ideas and beliefs with another person, especially when discussing something important to you. During the next couple of days consciously listen for the word **but** entering your conversations. Whether you or somebody else uses the word **but**, notice how it effects the dialogue and the mood of the conversation.

You can replace the word **but** with **and** while adding additional information. Recognize the person's right to their opinion and agree with or respect their position while adding additional information.

> Person A says *"It's a nice day."*
> Person B responds *"I agree **and** I heard it might rain later."*
> Person A now has to evaluate and respond to the new information.

When we evaluate who wins in any conflict we decide and identify who loses the least or who got hurt the least. Regardless of who is the winner both got hurt or lost. It becomes a matter of degree. The word **but** leads to conflict in communication; therefore, be aware of its impact whenever you choose to use the word *but* and replace it with more expansive and constructive language.

The word *why* may well be one of the most powerful words in our language. It is powerful because it always gets a response. The response can be either positive or negative.

Often the questioner asks *why* to request additional information. However, experience indicates the person being asked *why?* often responds negatively. The *why* question is often interpreted as challenging or nonaccepting which creates conflict and motivates *because* answers. This *why-because* dialogue tends to become a no-win loop and shuts down any effective conversation. Many people believe this no-win loop is created in childhood and develops a pattern of noncommunication triggered by the word *why*. Illustrating this conditioning process, I wonder if the following conversation sounds familiar.

> Child asks, *"Can I have some candy?"*
> Parent responds, *"No."*
> Child asks, *"Why?"*
> Parent responds, *"Because I said so!"*

My belief is that the negative response to the question *why* has two motivations. The first is the word *why* is interpreted as an attack on the authority or character of the person being questioned. Person A makes a statement and Person B responds with the question, *"Why?"* Person A's internal dialogue goes something like this: Don't you know who is in charge? Don't you have faith in my ability and opinions? Don't you recognize my value? This internal dialogue motivates the negative and defensive response.

The second motivation for a negative response occurs because the question *Why?* challenges the value or accuracy of Person A's statement and directs Person A to validate their own beliefs and the accuracy of their maps of the world. Seemingly people state information, ideas, or opinions which actually represent their own walls and they don't consciously understand why they have these rules and beliefs. They have never consciously questioned or evaluated these issues and proceed directly from stimulus to response. Sometimes the best defense is a good offense; therefore, negative response.

The words *but* and *why* can create conflicts in our communication. These conflicts tends to shut off sharing of ideas and information which can lead toward positive conclusions, expansion, and growth.

Another category of language which is becoming more prevalent and pervasive in our society is the use of vulgarity or curse words. What concerns me is the understanding that words indicate internal representations. Some words always seem to have negative representations reflecting anger, hate, or a lack of respect for anything. Often the use of these words becomes a habit, yet whenever they enter our language patterns they distort our representations of reality and the meaning of our communication.

Think about a person you love or respect. Imagine saying to that person "I really love you" or "I really respect you." Get a sense of your internal feelings when you say the words. Now repeat the process saying "I really F---ing love you" or "I really F---ing respect you." Notice how the addition of one word drastically affects your internal representation and the value and intent of the message.

These vulgar negative words are becoming more and more common in our society. We experience this language every day written in books, magazines, papers, and on the walls of our buildings. We also hear this language in movies, television, radio, walking through the malls or schools, and from our families and friends. Developing the pattern of using this language changes how we see the world; therefore, changing how we create our reality. This language lacks respect and distorts both our internal and external communication.

Become consciously aware of the words you choose. They represent the description and interpretation assigned to the raw data at the subconscious level as we transfer it to our conscious level of thinking. The words we choose to represent our inner feelings can be expansive and promote growth or they can be the building blocks of our walls which can limit our options and confine us within nonsupportive restrictive loops.

When I was twenty-three years old I was diagnosed as having an eye disorder called keratoconus, a deterioration of the corneal tissue. In 1975 I had a cornea transplant on my right eye and for several days after surgery both eyes were bandaged. During this time I had to deal with the experience and possibility of blindness. Surprisingly, I decided blindness would not be the worst thing that could happen and I realized how often my vision biased how I interpreted my world, especially the people. During this period without vision people were not short or tall, thin or fat, attractive or unattractive, black or white;

they were just fellow human beings. I didn't predetermine what to expect or classify or label them with words.

The surgery was effective and I came away from the experience with some valuable personal understandings and insights. I realized how generalizations and classifications of people create walls that limit my options and develop false maps of the territory.

I wonder how often the words we use to define people, including ourselves, limit our choices and direct inappropriate and nonsupportive behavior. Most prejudice toward any group throughout the world seems to start by generalizing and classifying the group and then assigning names to it. Next we link emotions like hate, fear, revenge, and other negative feelings to the names. This process restricts our ability to see people as individuals or human beings and all we see is a group which has negative internal representations.

Allow me to ask you a question. *If we consciously change our words can we also change the walls those words create?*

Which of the following statements do you think give me the most choices?

I am a white man, husband and father, who wants to make a positive difference.

or

I am a person who wants to make a positive difference, a husband and father, and I happen to be white.

Our self-description reflects how we internally represent ourselves; therefore, how we relate to the world. We need to consciously listen to our own words and identify those which establish walls that limit our choices and create inner conflict. Breaking through these walls will expand our ability to become the person we choose.

Thoughts for consideration

Consider the relationship between satisfaction and expectation.

There are two young men working at the same job. One comes from a very poor environment and the other is the son of the owner of the local newspaper.

The first young man has a dream of being a writer for his local newspaper. He attends college while working full time to pay his bills. He gets his degree in Journalism and finally gets an opportunity in the editorial department of the local newspaper.

The second young man has everything he wants and attends the finest college with all expenses paid by his wealthy father. He expects to someday take over his father's newspaper so he gets a degree in Journalism. His father wants him to learn the business so he starts in the editorial department.

Who do you think gets the most personal satisfaction from writing for the editorial department?

More effective things to ask rather than the question **Why?**

I don't understand, can you give me an example?

Can you explain it differently?

That's very interesting, can you tell me more?

Can you tell me how you came to that conclusion, idea or belief?

Similar to the word **but**, *we want to recognize the person's right to their opinion or agree with and respect their position while we request additional information.*

112

Do you believe the words you use can restrict how you interpret reality?

Does your language change depending on your mood? Does it change depending on who you are talking with?

How often have you heard or used the phrase, "I am doing the best that I can." It seems harmless enough, yet I believe it is very restrictive.

Before you use this phrase, you have to internally believe that you can do no better. This thinking eliminates the possibility of learning and attempting different approaches. Actually, this phrase is another way of saying "I give up" and it justifies your nonperformance.

Being Prejudice = Limiting choices

The need to belong to a group in society seems consistent for all people. Members of any group in society share some similar characteristics and usually share a set of beliefs and rules. One way to restrict the membership of this homogeneous group from considering the qualities of another group is to identify the other available groups and assign lessor or unequal value to them. The effect is discounting that group's beliefs, values, ideas, culture, and any other qualities associated with them. The members of the first group do not consider the possibility of learning from or accepting the second group and often do not consider them equal as human beings. Once we establish the belief that the other homogeneous group is not equal as human beings, we can behave toward them in very inhuman ways.

113

When we associate negative emotions like anger, hate, fear, resentment, revenge, or danger to the above situation it ignites the capacity of man's inhumanity to man.

Think of some examples of when assigning specific distinctions to a group allowed reducing that group to less than a human status. Consider events such as slavery, Native Americans, the Holocaust, the ethnic cleansing in Bosnia, the fighting and killing in Northern Ireland, or perhaps the violence and killing on the streets of America because of gang affiliation.

When we lose sight of the fact that we are all human beings sharing the same planet, the negative results are amazing. I do not believe I will ever understand man's capacity for inhumanity to man. For me it represents the dark side of the human experience. When we use the differences among people to justify less than human consideration and behavior toward them, we lose the ability to learn and grow by exploring the possibilities of our differences.

Being prejudice = limiting choices

Self description

Write a description of yourself. Be as clear as possible using as many descriptive words as necessary. Write as if you are describing yourself to someone you have never met in another part of the world.

Self description: _____

_____
_____
_____
_____

List the descriptive words in the order they appear in your self description in column one.

Column 1	Column 2

Evaluate your descriptive words and the order you used them to describe yourself. Do any of these words have a tendency of limiting your options or have any negative aspects? Notice which words are just objective observation and which words identify purpose and meaning in your lives. My example, "I am a white man, husband and father, who wants to make a positive difference." The words, "white man, husband and father" are objective observations. "A person who wants to make a positive difference" identifies purpose and meaning in my life. Changing the order of my description changes the focus of my attention about what is important in my life. This shift can allow me to see more opportunities to direct my life where I want it to go.

Write your descriptive words in column 2 in the order of importance.

Now write your new self description which may more accurately describe who you are.

New self description _____
_____
_____
_____
_____
_____
_____

chapter nine

Thoughts

Consistently I notice how thoughts are directly related to our reality and that everything in our lives started with a thought. Using our five senses we continuously collect information into our subconscious and then retrieve the desired data for evaluation at the conscious level of thinking. Our internal representations of these thoughts can be visual, auditory, or kinesthetic depending on our individual systems. We then use words and language to share these thoughts with others.

This understanding led me to some very interesting questions. What impact do internal language and beliefs have on our reality? How do we choose which information we bring to the conscious level? How do we interpret that information?

Apparently external thoughts and beliefs can have a strong impact on how we construct our reality and choose our behavior. These external thoughts and beliefs, which may not be correct, can develop into generalizations which become our point of view in identifying the territory. We then create our maps based upon that viewpoint.

Let me give an example using a cliche I have often heard, especially in business. "Don't work hard, work smart." I interpret this idea as meaning if you can be smarter than or outsmart others, you can get results without hard work or find smarter ways to work eliminating hard work. This idea may seem harmless, yet I wonder how many people have become intrigued with this cute shortcut point of view and it generated a work ethic that led to failure.

I get annoyed with this phrase because I believe it is misleading and I have yet to meet a person who works stupid on purpose. We can all learn more and educate ourselves toward more effective use of our ability. Maximizing our ability takes hard work and working as smart as we are capable toward our desired outcomes.

Our point of view has tremendous impact on how we perceive reality. Scarcity and abundance are two opposite points of view which affect how we identify options. By having a point of view of scarcity we will identify few or no acceptable options which lead to few or no results. Often this point of view leads us to giving up and generally feeling like a victim of some unidentified force. Having a point of view of abundance we will identify many workable options which produce abundant results.

Consciously recognizing the general perspective of our point of view allows more individual choice. Groups also have a general point of view which often starts with the leaders of the group. I believe the foremost problem in our country today is that we have developed a common consciousness which has a scarcity point of view and it impacts on how we identify and evaluate our options. Many sources of information like newspapers, magazines, television, and radio consistently focus on what is wrong and not working or negative in our society. This general focus tends to encourage the scarcity point of view.

In 1992 Bill Clinton was elected to replace George Bush as the President of the United States. How successful do you think Bill Clinton's campaign would have been if he identified and focused attention on the things President Bush accomplished and did well?

What if you are in charge of your local school system and are attempting to obtain additional funding for your programs from your state. Would you focus all your attention and conversations on the things that were successful and positive about your system? Probably not.

The unfortunate irony is by focusing attention on what is negative or not working, while attempting to secure resources to improve the current situation, we sometimes create an atmosphere of scarcity. This atmosphere restricts our believing in the existence of any effective options and short-circuits our efforts. The intentions are good but the outcome can be disabling.

I believe our country is now more prepared and capable of competing in the world market and creating a strong economy than in any other period in history. To accomplish this we must first expand our options and move away from thinking in terms of scarcity and create our future in an atmosphere of abundance.

Another area affected by this viewpoint of scarcity is the educational system. I am concerned about consistently hearing how bad our schools have become. I believe any person in this country with a sincere desire to get an education could not be stopped from attaining it. We have too often been conditioned to give the responsibility of educating our children to school systems and have dismissed the individual's desire and responsibility for learning.

A child who continually hears that the education system has let them down and the available education will not provide the tools necessary to build a good future cannot be held totally responsible for his or her attitudes. I am not saying our schools do not need change and improvement to keep up with the ever-growing changes in the world. I do believe the scarcity atmosphere reduces options for our youth and restricts their belief in education as the best way to prepare for the future.

Let me ask you a question. Does your reality generate your thoughts or do your thoughts generate your reality? I am not sure which one comes first or if either one comes first every time. We must keep guard at the entrances to our minds and become aware of the foundation and construction of our thoughts. We will always be influenced by external factors but other people's truth and reality may not be correct for us.

Illustrating this concept, let us consider movies and television. How many people do you think have established role models or acceptable patterns of behavior by watching movies and television? How many people have identified what they want in life from this media? The problem is that many times these life styles and role models are make-believe and not available in the real world.

Let me ask another question. Is it a coincidence that vulgarity, violence, and a general lack of respect for other people seem more common in the movies and television and these same behaviors and attitudes are growing in our society?

Thoughts possess an energy of their own. Whenever a thought comes into your world, take it inside and see how it feels. Ask yourself if it is consistent with and supportive of who you are. If it fits, it will become part of you and if it doesn't then let it go. Harboring thoughts that don't support you can only lead you in the wrong direction.

Thoughts for consideration

Identify some of your thoughts that may restrict or expand how you experience the world.
For example:
> *I am doing the best that I can.*
> *I can't expect much in my life, look where I was born.*
> *This is America, anything is possible.*
> *What the mind can conceive and believe, it can achieve.*

Review your thoughts and identify if they lead to a point of view of abundance or scarcity.

In today's world there is so much attention given to what is not working and what is wrong in our society that it is sometimes hard to focus on what is right. I believe this tendency is undermining the spirit of many people in our country.

What do you think about the current state of the world, our country, your school, state, community, family, or life?

PASS IT ALONG TIMES TWO

<u>The power of TIMES TWO</u> *Please consider working for me for 30 days and choose which of the following pay plans you prefer.*

Plan #1 $100,000 for the 30 days

Plan #2 Your pay starts with one penny for the first day and doubles (X2) each day for 30 days.

Day 1 $.01   Day 2 $.02   Day 3 $.04   Day 4 $.08
Day 5 $.16   Day 6 $.32   etc.

If you picked plan #1 you get $100,000
If you picked plan #2 you get $5,368,709.12

Now which plan would you pick?   TIMES TWO is very powerful!

PASS IT ALONG *Starting today, become aware each day of doing two caring and considerate things for another person while expecting nothing back in return. When the person says "Thank You" simply respond with "Your welcome, Pass It Along Times Two" and briefly explain the concept. If the chain continues, on the 30th day 536,870,912 people will have someone do a caring and considerate thing for them while expecting nothing back in return. That is more than two caring and considerate things for every person living in America. Will this make the world a better place?*

*Seemingly there is little chance of the chain continuing for the full 30 days; however, we have no way of knowing how far it will go and what positive impact it will have on the world. Certainly, the focus of **PASS IT ALONG TIMES TWO** will affect how we interact with the people we encounter and **we will make the world a better place.***

My number one peeve is when people commit to do something or promise to do something and never do it. I find many people talk a better game than they play.

Do you live in the world of "Do as I say, not as I do" or are you a person who walks your talk?

The most effective leadership is leadership by example. Can you improve your world by living your life as an example?

Do you live by the Golden Rule: "Do unto other as you would have them do unto you."

How would thinking about PASS IT ALONG TIMES TWO every day impact your behavior toward other people?

chapter ten

Metaprograms

EVALUATION & BEHAVIOR TENDENCIES

Metaprograms are patterns which reflect our tendencies or our point of view, as we construct our maps. These tendencies can become so strong they create walls by not allowing us to expand our options and behavior. Remember: *if you continue to do the same things, in the same way, you will get the same results.*

There is no right or wrong, good or bad in metaprograms and they are often context related which indicates we have different patterns for different situations. Personally, I found learning and understanding metaprograms supplied me with additional insight into my thought patterns. These insights allow me to notice myself running a pattern and shift my point of view to a different perspective which usually changes and expands my options.

The following are some metaprograms I find most insightful and useful in identifying personal tendencies.

Direction: moving toward - moving away
The motivation behind the direction metaprogram is usually moving toward pleasure or gain and away from pain or loss.

Consider this situation: Two people go three times a week to an exercise program. The first person goes because it makes her feel energized, healthy, and in general, good about herself. She is moving toward a healthy body. The second person goes because he is afraid of getting fat or sickly and does not want other people to think of him as lazy. He is moving away from ill health and laziness.

Ask yourself: *What do I want in life? in a job? from my family? or any thing else in your life?* Notice which direction is indicated in your answer. Identifying your direction tendency gives you some additional understandings about what motivates your actions.

Possibility or necessity
When identifying and evaluating an option, are we attracted by the possibility offered by our available choices, or are we forced to change.

Consider two people looking for a new job. The first person wants to better himself and is attracted to jobs that offer great possibility for growth and expansion. The second person is looking for another job because he cannot live on his current income or the career is a dead end. This person may even be out of work and needs money.

126

Ask yourself the question: *Why did I choose my current job? or whatever choices you have made in your life?* The answer will indicate what motivated your previous choices; possibility or necessity. People who are motivated by possibility tend to feel more in control of their lives and search for new options. People motivated by necessity tend to feel directed by their environment and do the best they can with whatever comes their way. They may say things like "If it ain't broke, don't fix it."

Internal or external frame of reference

While evaluating anything in your life do you just know inside what is right or when you have done a good job, or do you evaluate from the feedback you receive from external sources and other people's opinion. What impact does feedback from friends, associates, family, or managers have upon your self-evaluation?

Who validates your worth, value, or performance as being good or bad, effective or ineffective, or right or wrong? I find this question of validation very important in identifying tendencies which create walls. We may be more influenced by external sources then we consciously recognize. I do not want to imply that either frame of reference, internal or external, is correct. I do want you to identify how each affect your life and which is your tendency.

Convincer metaprogram

This metaprogram describes how we are convinced or accept things to be real or not real, true or false. This metaprogram relates back to our representation systems of visual, auditory, or kinesthetic. Do we have to see something to believe it, or can we just hear about something, or do we have to actually experience something before we validate and accept its existence?

Consider the ability of people riding a bicycle. How are we convinced that people can ride bicycles?

Do we have to see someone riding a bicycle?
Can someone tell us that people ride bicycles?
Do we have to actually ride a bicycle ourselves?

The second part of the convincer metaprogram is the number of times we have to see, hear, or personally experience something before we believe and accept it into our reality.

This convincer metaprogram allows us to understand our tendencies directing how we collect information and create our reality using our five senses. Knowing our primary tendency allows us to evaluate information from a different point of view; thus, expanding our options.

Sorting by self or sorting by others

When evaluating any situation or information which enters your world, do you evaluate from how the information affects you personally, or do you consider how the information affects the people around you or people in general. This is not to identify a person as selfish or self-centered; rather, to point out how we focus our attention on the data we collect and how we respond to events in our lives.

Many times while driving or interacting with others I have become annoyed when cut off by another driver or when people appear uncaring or rude, as if I had no value and do not deserve common courtesy. I now realize I don't need to take it personally. Usually these people are just sorting by self and absorbed in their own thoughts and are not consciously aware that I even exist in their world at that moment. Whenever these types of events now occur, I tend to laugh because I know I have exhibited similar behavior to others while absorbed in my own thoughts.

Sorting by self or sorting by others can have a tremendous impact on our behavior and how we interact with others. It also represents a strong point of view while creating our maps. How do you sort your attention and what impact does it have on your world?

Relationship metaprogram

This metaprogram reflects how we make sense of new information or situations and identify how they fit into our reality. In this metaprogram we are considered either matchers or mismatchers, depending upon whether we focus our attention on the similarities or the differences. Do you focus on what is the same or on what is different about new information in relationship to your current map of the world?

How would you describe the relationship between these three coins?

There are four categories of responses reflecting various points of view.

1. *Sameness people* will see everything that is alike. They are all coins, they are all round, and they are all currency. They will not notice any differences.

2. *Sameness with exception people* will first see the things that are alike and then notice some things that are different. All are round, coins, and currency, yet they are also different sizes and have different values.

3. *Difference with exception people* will first see the things that are different and then notice the things that are the same. The coins are different sizes, different values, and different engravings, yet they are all coins.

4. *Difference people* will only see the differences. The coins are all different and don't have any relationship to each other.

Sameness people making sense of new information focus their attention on the elements which are similar to their own map of the territory. Sameness people usually don't like changes in their lives and tend to have agreeable personalities.

Difference people making sense of new information focus their attention on the elements which are different. These people often question everything before they accept it as true and appropriate for their world.

Throughout my business career I have often been classified as negative and not a team player. This always puzzled me because I believed myself very positive and always a team player. I also wondered about why when a positive comment or observation was appropriate you had to wait in line to be heard, but when a question or negative concern which may be accurate or helpful seemed appropriate nobody spoke up. I often found myself in the latter category.

When I learned about metaprograms, especially matching and mismatching, I finally understood my labels. I realized I am a mismatcher with exception and therefore make sense of the world by first focusing on differences. I also tend to question everything. Additionally, I used words like *why* and *but* which I now realize can lead to conflict. These new understandings about my tendencies has identified some patterns I wasn't aware existed and expanded my options and behavior.

Metaprograms are very useful in consciously understanding how we evaluate our world and construct our personal reality. Whenever we identify tendencies which can create walls that restrict our ability to identify and evaluate options we are able to escape their confinement.

Have you ever met someone you just don't like or feel uncomfortable being around? Many times these people have different tendencies than ours and they see the same world differently. We tend to like people who have things in common with us and share a similar map of the territory. Metaprograms not only support us in understanding how we create our reality but assist us in understanding and appreciating how other people see the world. This expands our perspective by exposing us to a different point of view outside of our own reality. Discovering your tendencies and understanding how metaprograms motivate your choices gives you the knowledge and power to really start your engines, fuel your fire, and create the inner excitement to supercharge your life.

Thoughts for consideration

Metaprograms are another part of the puzzle as to what we choose to bring to our conscious level of thinking from all the data we collect through the five senses. Identifying and understanding our metaprograms supplies us with additional information about where we focus our attention and how we create our reality.

How does your preference in each metaprogram affect where and how you focus your attention?

For example:

> *How will you value education if you move toward?*
> *What will you focus your attention on?*
> *How will you see your options?*

> *How will you value education if you move away-from?*
> *What will you focus your attention on?*
> *How will you see your options?*

chapter eleven

Goals and How They Work

Imagine you are walking along a quiet beach just before sunrise. It is late August. The air is warm and you feel the warm water on your feet as you walk along in the shallow surf. You smell the salty air and listen to the waves breaking on the beach and the seagulls calling the sunrise as they await their morning feeding. As you walk you watch the morning sky becoming brighter and brighter. Anticipating the arc of the sun breaking the surface of the horizon your mind soars with feelings of freedom and possibilities in your life. You are absorbed with the beauty of nature and how wonderful life can be when you step on a shell and cut your foot. It is amazing how fast your attention shifts from the beauty of sunrise over the ocean to the pain in your foot. Immediately you attend to your cut and when you once again look up the sun is almost completely above the horizon and you have missed the wondrous sight. While slowly walking home, where do you think you will be looking, up toward the sky pondering all of life's wonders or down at the sand avoiding shells?

Let me ask you a question. Can you feel your big toe touching the front of your shoe or the floor where it is resting? Can you feel your weight on your buttocks resting on your chair? Were you consciously aware of feeling your toe or buttocks before I directed your attention to that specific area? Probably not, yet the physical stimulus was constantly there.

The mind is constantly receiving thousands of bits of information through the five senses. Most of this information is received at the subconscious level and becomes part of the data pool I referred to earlier. We then use the filters of distortion, deletion, and generalizations to select what information is appropriate for our conscious awareness.

Our conscious mind has limited capacity and cannot deal with all the data collected. Work done by George Miller on the limits of our capacity to process information identified the conscious level of the human mind has the capacity for only 7 plus or minus 2 bits of information at any one time.

The ability to focus our attention on what we believe important at a certain time directs the process identifying what to retrieve from the subconscious data pool for the conscious mind. As I direct you to feel your big toe or buttocks you become consciously aware of that specific stimulus which is always present, but has been either deleted or generalized out of your conscious awareness. The same thing occurs when you step on a sharp shell and you direct your attention to what has become more important at that moment.

I believe goals work in the same manner. By clearly identifying and focusing on your goals, you create a set of filters which directs the appropriate information supporting the attainment of those goals to your conscious mind. You take control over the filtering process which sorts, evaluates, and assigns value to the collected information.

While attending seminars or working with various books I often wrote out my goals, yet I always seemed to come up short of identifying goals which really added excitement to my life. I now understand and believe that identifying meaningful goals takes a little more conscious effort than just making a list of what sounds good or accepting other people's goals and expectations as my own. Remember, I consider this the human paradox. We are conditioned to conform and breaking this thinking pattern, which will allow us to identify goals based upon our inner self-reality, is often difficult.

Many of the concepts and ideas I have shared in this book are the elements of the self-knowledge and self-direction necessary to establish meaningful goals. The kind of goals that add purpose and meaning to your life, creates excitement about getting up each day, and keep you going when things get difficult or don't seem to be going your way.

When establishing goals they should be congruent with your current reality or map of the territory. Recognize that as you grow through your life you will gather new knowledge and information which may alter your reality and your truths. This personal growth will affect who you are and necessitate frequent evaluation of your stated goals.

Let's identify and consider some elements of meaningful goal creation. Clearly identify your values and recognize how they direct and evaluate your behavior. Often people establish goals that are in conflict with the essence of who they are or their core values. Internal conflict sabotages efforts towards the attainment of the goal and can create feelings of failure. I believe the exercise of listing and prioritizing your values is essential to effective goal-setting. Without consciously considering your values, which direct all your behavior, how can you accurately identify and evaluate any goal?

Goals must be stated only in the positive, that is, what I do want as opposed to what I do not want. If I say to you "Don't look down!", the first thing your mind does is make a representation of looking down and then attempts not to do it. If I say "Look up!", your mind makes a representation of looking up and then naturally moves in that direction. Another example: Close your eyes and don't think about what an elephant looks like. Did you see the elephant?

Negatively stated goals can be very destructive and undermine our effort because whatever the mind thinks about will expand into our reality. When we think in positive terms, we get positive results. When we think in negative terms, we get negative results.

Answer the question: *What do I really want?* Identify and clearly write your goals specific enough for another person to fully understand including elements such as time frames, amounts, and qualities. This exercise of writing out your goals is essential in goal-setting. Think back to our discussion about Joe the Bartender. Problems not clear enough to share with another person using language are not clear enough to address. The same understanding is applicable to goals. Goals not clear enough to share with another are not clear enough to accurately focus on and effectively work toward. These vague goals will never supply the excitement necessary for their accomplishment.

The idea of specifically identifying elements such as time frame, amounts, and quantities create a clearer understanding of the goal and identifies when you have achieved it. Adding short term goals to the big picture or final outcome goals allows you to recognize the steps along the way and appreciate your progress. These short term steps are very helpful when you hit a snag or have a discouraging day or event.

Ask yourself: *What additional information, learning, education, and skills must I acquire to accomplish my goal?* Your goals must be achievable in your reality and not just false dreams, possibly created externally. Upon identifying your goal clearly recognize what price you have to pay and be prepared to pay the price for your achievement.

Your goals must be about yourself and your life and cannot depend upon other people's effort or accomplishments for their achievement. Goals depending on other people's performance put us out of control of the attainment of the goal and often lead to frustration and failure to accomplish the goal.

Here you are. You have identified and clearly written your goals. They are specifically stated; therefore, you have an evidence procedure to identify their accomplishment. You believe you know the additional tools you need and are prepared to attain them, but somehow you still don't have the excitement. The question you have to answer for yourself is **What is stopping me?** This may be the time you realize you are confined by your walls.

I believe this is when goal-setting falls apart, but have faith and hope. You have been establishing these walls all of your life and it may take some effort to break through to the other side. Identifying the existence of the walls is the first critical step. Goals that lack inner excitement and don't add meaning and purpose to your life may be the wrong goals, or you believe you cannot really achieve them.

Fear of loss or pain and desire for gain or pleasure motivate most, if not all, of the choices we make in our lives. Some odd and unidentified force seems to create more impact by fear of loss or pain as opposed to desire for gain or pleasure. These fears are often the root cause for us not getting excited about our goals.

Once at a seminar the question was asked, "What are you afraid of?" We were to tell our fears to the person standing next to us. At that moment I realized what I was afraid of was fear itself. Think about fear. In life there are two types of events, those we have control over and those we have no control over. Fear not only restricts us from identifying which type of event we are dealing with, but often paralyzes us from responding to the event. We are then victims of the events, many of which we can control. The fear blocks our ability to identify and evaluate options. I now comprehend the old saying, "The only thing to fear is fear itself."

Check inside yourself for any fears, perhaps of failure, pain, embarrassment, rejection, or other restrictions limiting your excitement for your goals. As you identify your fears evaluate their truth and value. Compare them to what is positive and supportive about your goals. Use the Ben Franklin evaluation process to write out the pros and cons about your goals and notice the positive outweighing the negative. Fears are often just illusions or products of your walls and when you consciously focus on them they surrender their power to control your behavior.

Review your goals looking for any conflicts between the goals and your reality or map of the territory. Conflicts can be just below the conscious level and need to be identified and eliminated. Either the goal is not appropriate or your map needs some adjustment. Recheck your values relative to your goals. Often goals are motivated by external influences and are in conflict with your core values. For example, you may want to be a very successful salesperson, but you have a hard time with rejection. This will lead to definite internal conflict. Review your metaprograms and the language you use while thinking about or writing your goals. Look for any limiting beliefs which restrict your ability to identify meaningful goals or your ability to commit to the goals you have chosen.

While you continue to identify and clarify your goals, remember, your walls may be solidly constructed; therefore, be patient and don't expect an immediate break through. Every day pay attention to the small incremental steps which take you where you want to be. Read your goals each day to reinforce the filters and where you want to focus attention. This directs what information will be delivered to your conscious mind. As you focus daily on your goals you may be surprised how they attract new and supportive information. You will notice new insights and observations which previously escaped your conscious awareness.

Continue consciously focusing on your goals and the process builds upon itself and becomes stronger with each new supportive discovery. The more of yourself you apply to the achievement of the goal, the more it becomes part of who you are and the more you build the excitement which creates purpose and meaning to your life.

Remember my definition of success: *Success is living every day of your life in the direction of your own goals, dreams, and ideals.* Having no goals is like sailing without any control of the sails. Your destination depends totally on which way the wind is blowing. Having goals gives you command of your ship and you control the sails no matter which way the wind happens to blow. You can now set a course toward an exciting and chosen future.

Thoughts for consideration

I offer the message handed down by the 2nd century Roman emperor Marcus Aurelius, "Anything the mind can conceive and believe, it can achieve."

People who do not attain their goals always have excuses. People who do attain their goals don't need any excuses.

I once read: Circumstances don't make the man, they expose him.

The following is the results of a study to identify why people fail.
> *#1   They try to be something they are not.*
> *#2   They do not learn to handle stress.*
> *#3   They build a case against themselves before they start.*

How will each of these reasons undermine your efforts in attaining your goals?

Is it possible that fear is a valuable friend?
> *In nature it is extremely important for animals to be in touch with their survival instincts. One of the most important instincts is fear which signals them about potential danger. We should learn to consider fear our friend. Recognize that our fears are only signals about possible danger. Our fears allow us to identify the possible danger and make the proper adjustments to eliminate the threat.*

What I want in my life

The first thing to do is identify and write what you want in your life considering the elements discussed in the chapter. Next write some thoughts about the following questions:

> *What will it do for me?*
> *How will I know when I get it?*
> *What stops me now?*
> *What do I need in order to get it?*

Write as many goals as you want. The more goals you desire and work toward, the more exciting your life.

What I want in my life:

chapter twelve

Breaking Through Walls

The boundaries we establish for our minds are the greatest walls in our lives. Whether these walls are self-constructed or the result of the conditioning process of conforming to society, they still hold us in nonsupportive nonexpanding loops. They also restrict us from identifying more expansive growth-directed options.

The first step in breaking through your walls is to consciously recognize their existence. Notice yourself being stuck in the same old patterns that are not getting you the results you want in your life. Let us consider some things I believe useful in identifying and breaking through walls.

Logical progression of ideas and beliefs

Growing through life we continually expand our reality by building upon our current understanding of what we believe true. As we continue the process we become more and more confident and secure in the accuracy of our maps of the territory. What we believe to be true becomes our point of view and the filters we use in evaluating new information. These filters focus our attention on things which reinforce what we already believe. The following equation represents the process:

A=B   B=C   C=D   D=E   E=F   F=G   therefore A=G

Whenever we are not getting the results we want in our lives and we cannot identify the source of our nonsupportive pattern, the answer may lie at the base of this logical progression. Every time we reinforce a truth or belief it becomes more a part of who we are and our reality. Each reinforcement also distances us from the base truth which started the process. The longer it continues the harder it becomes to track back to the starting point and evaluate a lifetime of beliefs and decisions. Considering the progression of an idea or belief, based upon it's own accuracy, we now believe A=G. The question is: Was A accurate as the beginning truth?

Reflecting on my own life, I shared my pattern of never really attempting anything because if I didn't try, I could never fail, and then my father could never be right about my lack of ability. This logical progression of ideas and behavior consistently short-circuited my life and was based upon the possibility of my father's accuracy. Once I finally identified and focused on this wall I broke through to more supportive and expansive options.

Validation

The only person who can validate you and take responsibility for your life is you. A common wall I have observed is constructed when we allow other people's values and beliefs to direct our lives. People who care about us or those we interact with have opinions and expectations of how we should behave and create our reality. Their opinions and expectations are based upon their map of the world. Usually their intentions are well meaning, but they can lead us to establishing patterns of not listening to our own internal signals.

I find it useful to listen to other people because they interpret the territory from a different perspective than my own. Their perspective may well uncover things which I have overlooked or are outside of my walls. Consider external opinions as feedback and a resource for ideas and observations that you can evaluate while creating your own maps. Always remember, you are the only person living your life and only you are responsible for your choices. You are the only person who really knows what you want in and for your life.

A word of caution: Be aware that other people often take offense and become disappointed when you don't accept their ideas and suggestions. I often marvel how many people say, *Live and let live,* yet behave *Let me live and I will tell you how to live.*

Mind-Reading occurs when we think we know what another person is thinking or how they represent reality. How many times have you chosen not to ask a question or do something because you believed you already knew what the other person was thinking? How many times have you created walls limiting your options by mind-reading other people's reality? The truth is we can never be sure what another person is thinking. Often our mind-reads have no factual foundation and are created by our fears and false assumptions.

Another aspect of mind reading occurs when we predetermine how another person should behave or how they should see the world. Have you ever participated in this type of mind-read and then entered a nonproductive state of anger, frustration, disappointment, or other restrictive thinking pattern when the other person chooses to behave differently from how you determined they should? We create our own negative state by not recognizing we are mind-reading and not accepting the other person's choices. Many times we enter this restrictive state even though we never expressed our opinions or expectations to the other person. Ironically, the more we care about the other person, like a family member, the more this restrictive state creates walls that do not allow us to identify more accepting options.

Brainstorming is possibly the most effective technique for breaking through walls and expanding our reality. In mathematics we add the quantity of things to reach the total amount:

1person + 1 person + 1 person = 3 people

When adding thoughts the whole is usually greater than the sum of its parts:

1 person's thoughts + 1 person's thoughts + 1person's thoughts = something greater than 3 people's thoughts

What happens is person A shares a thought. Person B then expands upon the thought from their point of view or reality which adds to and expands person A's perspective. The process continues feeding on itself and expands the options available to all the participants. We benefit most from brainstorming when we consider each participant's point of view and reality as resources for us to identify and evaluate options currently outside of our maps of the world.

Whenever somebody doesn't agree with my position I consider their opinions as feedback from outside my perspective. When we participate in discussions reflecting total agreement, little expansion occurs. Debating any issue can be a very productive growth experience as long as we don't allow ego, the need to be right, or the need to win to block out our ability to understand what the other people bring to the debate.

In the final analysis we will decide what best supports us and fits into our world. Hopefully, the other people will do the same. The brainstorming exercise is very valuable for us to identify options and perspectives currently outside of our reality and can open passages through our walls.

Modeling is a powerful method of breaking through our walls. Locate someone who is already achieving the results you want in your life and model what they are doing. When possible, have a discussion with the person you are modeling and uncover and understand any and all information available concerning how they obtain the results you are interested in. Search for elements like values, beliefs, rules, patterns, goals, education, work habits, and preferences. In general, learn how they create their maps. You can then pattern your behavior accordingly and you will get similar results using your own abilities.

When a personal discussion is not available, learn from other sources such as their associates, books, magazines, news articles, taped interviews, personal appearances, and your own observations. Study their lives and their accomplishments. Even without personal discussion you can still gather enough information to pattern our behavior toward the desired results.

Here is a belief that may help you. Success and achievement leaves clues. When you identify and understand the clues you can construct a similar strategy to direct and support your attaining the results you desire.

Branching or mind maps is an effective technique to allow brainstorming within our own mind. Research has identified that the human brain has two hemispheres, each displaying a different type of thinking process. Nobody is totally left or right-brain, yet we do tend to have a dominant hemisphere.

Left-brain dominated individuals exhibit thinking patterns which are sequential, step by step, analytical, and somewhat matter-of-fact. Left-brain dominant people will usually organize their ideas on paper by listing the ideas in order.

Right-brain dominated individuals are spontaneous, visual, intuitive, and creative. Often right-brain dominant people write their ideas in no specific order with little attention to sequence.

Having a dominant hemisphere is a limitation because left-brain people use a step-by-step approach to list and write their thoughts and often do not tap into their creative and intuitive abilities. Right-brain people randomly write their feelings and thoughts, which may be very creative and intuitive, but lack enough structure to support a meaningful evaluation.

Branching or mind mapping allows both sides of your brain to successfully participate in creating a whole mind representation of an issue. Start with a blank piece of paper and in the middle draw a circle. In that circle identify the central issue you wish to expand. Allow your mind to brainstorm any ideas that could relate to the central issue. What you are doing is drawing information from your subconscious data pool. Draw lines like branches from a tree, starting at the central circle, with additional branches coming off the main branch. As you identify a key idea write it on one of the main branches using a short descriptive word or phrase to reflect the idea. Write additional thoughts supporting this key idea on the secondary branches. Notice how ideas motivate additional ideas and the process expands the central issue, similar to brain storming with others. As additional key ideas surface, write them on another branch and as secondary ideas surface write them on the secondary branches of the corresponding key idea branch.

Notice the involvement of both sides of your brain. This process satisfies the listing and sequential patterns of the left hemisphere and also allows the free expression of creative and random patterns of the right hemisphere. What is created is a whole brain evaluation.

I have supplied a sample which will clearly illustrate the process. My original mind map or branching exercise when I started writing this book was done on a 24 inch by 28 inch piece of construction board and I filled almost the entire space available.

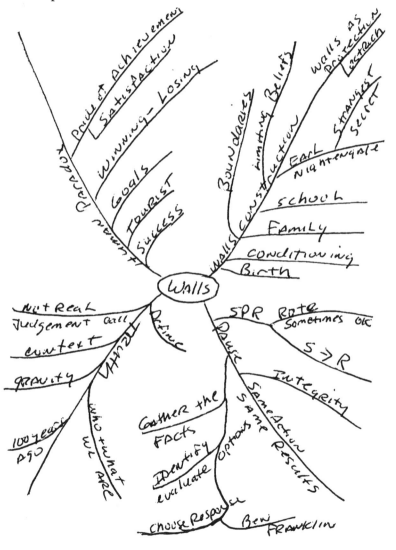

Twenty possibilities is another simple technique to tap into your subconscious data pool. Identify the central issue or problem you want to evaluate and every morning write 20 possible options or ideas which might relate to the stated issue. Let your mind go free and write anything that enters your conscious awareness. Even consider the direct opposite of any original possibility.

To illustrate this technique, consider the issue of losing weight:

1-- eat less
2-- eat more (better foods)
3--exercise daily
4--walk every morning
5-- join a exercise program with a friend
6-- take up square dancing
etc.
etc.
20 -- run a marathon

You must commit to write 20 possibilities each day because this will direct you to stretch and draw out the appropriate options. Continue this exercise every day until you have sufficient options. We already have the answers to most of our questions. All we have to do is bring them to the conscious level and discover one we can accept, which will effectively direct the appropriate behavior.

Whenever I *research and read* any topic, I am always amazed how much information is available. Whatever interest or idea we have has probably been evaluated by someone before us. Often they have written about their observations and beliefs to share with anyone who follows them. Reading is a great resource to expand our awareness of information and options outside of our world.

Many people appear to have difficulty identifying what they want to do with their lives, especially when choosing a career. They can use mind mapping to brainstorm many options that seem to offer interesting possibilities and then research each idea to identify and understand the potential of each possibility and what it takes to proceed in that direction.

My son wasn't sure what he wanted to do when he graduated from high school, yet he thought he might like to become involved in making films about wildlife. He started at a local school during the summer and the dream started to take shape as he became exposed to film options. He then researched the field and the more he learned the more the dream became real and the possibilities continued to expand. He is now starting a program which will allow him to follow his dream and his interest and excitement could not be higher. In the beginning he was trapped in his walls of ignorance about options. As his research and reading continued, so did the expansion of his choices and the excitement about the possibilities.

Once I was told that reading is the key to knowledge. I also have been told that knowledge is power. The first statement I believe true, but knowledge is not power. Using the knowledge to direct and support your efforts toward achieving your goals, dreams, and ideals is power.

Last but not least is breaking the common wall of *negative or scarce thinking.* Whenever you find things not going your way, stop for a minute and count your blessings. This sounds pretty simple, yet it really works. Remember from our thoughts on goals, if you think in negative terms you will get negative results. You cannot build an exciting and meaningful future focusing your attention on what you don't have or limitations in your life. Focus your attention on what is good and working in your life and it will expand.

Thoughts for consideration

Knowing something is different than believing in the possibility of something. When you were a child you may have believed you could ride a bicycle because you saw everybody else riding. When you actually got on the bike and rode it, the belief changed to knowing you can ride a bicycle. This knowing is now yours for the rest of your life.

Sometimes we get so caught up in what we believe true and right that we are unable to consider any other possibilities. We must always remain open to evaluating what we believe and what we know by considering other people's maps of the territory. It is a win-win situation. We will either reinforce our current beliefs or gather new information to adjust our focus.

When you compare yourself to another person you are still yourself. In our society it is common to judge a person by how they compare to others rather than accepting them as an unique individual. Comparing yourself to others doesn't change or improve your abilities and can lead to developing walls which may restrict your choices. In the history of mankind and for the rest of time there is not, or ever will be, anybody just like you experiencing your life.

Could some of your beliefs and accepted truths be the result of bad comparisons?
I am a good person. I am a bad person. I am a smart person. I am not so smart.

Think about times you were guilty of getting upset when somebody did not do what you expected and times when others got upset with you for the same reason. Consider past experiences with your family, teachers, coaches, boyfriend / girlfriend, husband / wife.

Would more open effective communication eliminate some of these situations?

chapter thirteen

Emotional State Control

Have you ever wondered how other people internally experience feelings of love, hate, excitement, accomplishment, fear, possibility, loss, grief, or any other emotional state? We appreciate other people's emotional states by comparing them to how we would feel in a similar situation such as falling in love or the death of a loved one. We observe their outward expressions and behavior which indicate to us what is going on inside them, but we can never experience another's emotional state. This effort is our emotional mind-reading.

I believe when we come to our last moments of life we all want to look back over our lives and evaluate our existence as having purpose and meaning. This search for our purpose and meaning directs most of the choices we make during our lives.

Some years ago I read a book titled, <u>A Stone for Danny Fisher</u> by Harold Robbins. I don't recall the entire story but I will never forget the last line. Danny Fisher died and written on his tombstone is: "To live in the hearts we leave behind is not to die." This line changed my entire outlook about life and death. I believe we all want to live in the hearts and minds of the people we have touched during our lives. This represents to me the positive purpose and meaning of our existence.

Our internal emotional states are the drivers for all our choices and behavior. Every choice we make is motivated by how it makes us feel inside. We cannot give these feelings away or get them from another, but we can be influenced by other people's behavior.

Let's consider the state of love. Your internal representation of love may be different from mine, yet most agree it is a positive and highly charged emotion. Another person enters your world and their existence and behavior generate feelings inside you which you identify as love. These feelings motivate your positive caring behavior to the other person. The relationship grows and becomes stronger, building upon itself. In a sense, love can be considered a selfish emotion because we exhibit caring and very positive behavior toward another person motivated by how it makes us feel inside. It is our love and we are the only person who can experience its wonders.

We cannot control another person's behavior, yet their behavior can have a powerful impact on our internal states. Consider again the state of love. Have you ever experienced another person changing their behavior toward you and noticed it motivating a change in your state? Has this change diminished the wonderful internal high that accompanies the feeling of love? Applying the concept of walls, have we been conditioned to establish our internal state by external stimuli? Do we have to give up our wonderful internal feelings of love because others changed their minds?

My observations indicate the people who seem to get the most satisfaction from their lives are the ones who focus on their supportive and positive emotional states and avoid the negative and destructive states. You do have control over where you focus your attention and that allows you to control your emotional state.

These negative and destructive or nonsupportive states are often very sneaky as they enter your world. Notice the invasion and recognize you are not defenseless against the attack. Many of the ideas in this book support you in identifying and making choices in your life.

Have you ever been in a situation when an external stimulus seems to overwhelm you and take you out of control; perhaps in a heated argument, just before you have to speak in public, the loss of someone or something in your life, or physical pain? Catching ourselves in this state, we have to step back and regain control.

Meditation is a method of quieting the mind. A basic concept of meditating is that oxygen is a basic element of life; therefore, breathing is necessary for existence. I find a very simple meditation technique is to focus my attention on my breathing. Breathing in, I focus my attention on the air as the basic element of life, and breathing out, I focus on letting go of all negative energies. Inhale deeply, expanding your midsection. Hold the air for a short period and than exhale completely. Notice the tingling sensation all over your body. The degree and depth of the breathing meditation varies and you can increase your ability with practice.

Conscious breathing is directing your attention to your breathing and it is very useful whenever you are overwhelmed by an external stimuli. You can use it to ground yourself and regain control of your emotional state. Usually, shifting your attention to conscious breathing for only two or three breaths is enough to step back from the situation and maintain your control.

Conscious breathing is also useful when you feel physically or emotionally tired or flat. Focus your attention on inhaling full and deep breaths, holding the air in for a few seconds, and then exhaling completely. You can feel the rush of oxygen through out your body as it energizes your entire system.

Anchoring is a powerful technique to take advantage of the mind-body connection. The process of anchoring is to stimulate emotional states by using physical stimuli. Let's create an anchor for a high energy state so you can experience its effect.

Take a deep breath and feel the energy building in your body. As you exhale shout the word *YES!* loud and strong and notice how it adds more energy. Now every time you shout *YES!* clench your fist and squeeze tightly. Continue for eight or ten breaths and feel the energy growing. Take a break and relax for a few minutes.

Again take eight to ten deep breaths while clenching your fist and shouting *YES!* as you exhale, reaching the high energy state, and again relax. Continue through three or four cycles.

Now fire the physical anchor of just squeezing your fist and notice your entire body shifting to the high energy state. How did you do? Did you experience how it works? The more you reinforce the anchor the more effective it becomes. You can anchor any state you desire and call on it at will. The anchor must be the same every time and you need to establish different anchors for each desired state.

One of the anchored states I use is that of being grounded and feeling in balance with myself and in control of my choices. I entered the grounded state by using the conscious breathing technique to quiet my mind and relax. At the high point of the desired state, I created an anchor by pressing the thumb nail on my left hand into the front top of my left index finger. I reinforced the anchor by repetition. Now, whenever I fire the anchor, I feel the relaxation flow through my body.

We can also anchor to sounds, sights, or activities. When I was a small boy and learned to whistle, I noticed I could not be in a sad or bad mood and whistle at the same time. I don't know if the same experience is true for everyone; however, using this belief, I have reinforced this experience and it always works for me. Whenever I catch myself in a sad or bad mood, I have the choice to either focus on the mood and identify its message and the conflict it represents, or I can whistle and let the mood go away.

Considering the down-side of anchoring, I now realize that when I was young I anchored a lot of nonsupportive and negative emotions to my father's face and his angry looks. Whenever I looked into his face it fired my internal representations of feeling inadequate and disappointing to him. I didn't understand anchoring at that time and my father and I had a very strained relationship up until his death. I never really got to know the man and understand how he created his map of the world and I don't believe he ever really got to know me.

Advertisers use anchoring to motivate our emotional buying decisions. I hope you don't think manufacturers and distributors like Nike give the tremendous amounts of money to people like Michael Jordan and Bo Jackson just because they like them. Their motivation is for you to assign feelings of having great athletic abilities, talent, performance, and a high degree of success, which these athletes represent, to their products. They are influencing your buying decision using anchoring.

Throughout our lives what happens externally isn't as important as how we react and deal with the stimuli. We can control our internal emotional states. Focusing on the positive states empowers us with the mental attitude, energy, and enthusiasm to create the lives we want and identify and appreciate our true purpose and meaning.

Thoughts for consideration

What is the purpose and meaning for your life?

How do you want people to remember you when you are dead?

Everything we do is chosen because of how it makes us feel. To identify the feeling or emotional state ask: What do I get from that? Keep asking until you get to the feeling.

For example:

I go to work.	*What do I get from that?*
I get some money.	*What do I get from that?*
I pay my bills and buy food.	*What do I get from that?*
I am taking care of my family.	*What do I get from that?*
*I **feel good** about myself.*	

Think about anything you do in your life and by asking this question you will always get down to a feeling as the true motivation for your actions.

Remember, being responsible for your life includes being responsible for your emotional state.

Can you think of a time when external events directed your choices and behavior?
Can some people just push the right buttons to set you off?
Are there some situations which make you feel out of control? Inferior? Fearful?
Have you ever gotten to the point when you feel like you just can't take any more?

Sometimes people anchor emotional states unintentionally.
A young boy starts school. He has a hard time sitting still and he seems to have difficulty keeping up with what the other children are doing. Soon the teacher (wanting to help) starts exploring possible reasons and often discusses "the problem" with the parents. The boy anchors feelings of inferiority and failure to going to school. As he reinforces the anchors, school soon becomes a negative place and he enters his non-resourceful state whenever he goes there.

Another example of unintentional and restrictive anchors:
A man has a really bad day at work. The traffic on the way home is heavy and he gets into an argument with another driver who cuts him off. He walks into his home and starts complaining about his day to his wife. He is looking at his wife's face as he shares the events and experiences the negative emotional feelings. This man is

not happy and content with what he does for a living and this "Bitch Session" becomes a daily event.

In this type of situation, it is very common for the man to anchor the negative emotional feelings to his wife's face. She may well anchor his angry unhappy states to his face. Soon when they look at each other the negative emotional states return. These anchors can really undermine their marriage. Be aware of your emotional state and the impact of anchoring.

Anchoring values for state control

In Thoughts for consideration at the end of chapter six, I discuss the inmates at Graterford Correctional Institution and anchoring the experience of freedom to conscious breathing. This became a vehicle for them to use as a pattern interrupt when they catch themselves beginning to run an old pattern. They can call "Time out" and evaluate different options. It allows them to step back from a situation and not get caught up in the event.

This technique works with any value. I explained to the inmates that I use my highest value of Balance. I gave my experience as an example while explaining the exercise. Where I use the word Balance you can use any word that is meaningful to you.

Get into a comfortable position and close your eyes.

Take a few deep breaths, expanding your mid-section, which is how you should breath for maximum effect.

Notice the feeling of relaxation in your body as it increases with each breath.

With each breath focus on your value word and experience the feelings associated with it. Say your value word in your mind as you exhale.

What do you see when you experience Balance?
 I see the clear night sky, filled with so many stars it is hard to separate the stars from the sky.

What do you hear when you experience Balance?
 I hear crickets chirping and the wind gently moving the leaves in the trees.

What do you feel when you experience Balance?
 I feel at peace, safe, and free to just ponder the possibilities of my life.

 I explained to the inmates that they have anchored their desired state to deep breathing and the word. When they feel themselves losing control they can just take a deep breath, think of the value word, and the feelings associated with the state will flow into their bodies. I suggested they practice this technique for a few minutes each night before sleep and each morning before getting out of bed. The more you reinforce the anchor the more effective it becomes.
 As you practice and use this technique you will become aware of how much control you actually have over your emotional state.

chapter fourteen

The Context of the Book

I believe the unique essence of our humanity, which you may identify as our spirit, soul, intellect, free will, energy source, or whatever, does not have any physical properties and does not end with our physical death. I believe this essence has experienced life before humanity and will go to another life after our death.

Imagine asking a kindergarten child on their first day of school to solve a very advanced or previously unsolved mathematical equation appropriate for a person with a doctorate in that specific field. We may find one or two children in the world able to understand and solve the problem using very unique and unexplainable abilities. All the other children would not know where to start or have any concept of what we were asking. They don't have references or knowledge to understand the equation because it is far beyond their capacity at this stage of their development. Some of these children may someday work, study, and obtain a doctorate in that specific field, and only then will they have any possibility of completing the task.

Like the small child and the mathematical equation, we do not have the references or knowledge to understand and comprehend where our unique essence came from, and where it is going. Part of the human experience is living within the constraints of our humanity and understanding our unique essence is beyond our capacity.

While I was in college I became aware of the possibility of UFOs, and I now believe they exist. It seems to me, if life forms can reach our planet they must be further advanced than us because we cannot overcome the element of time and other human physical restraints which prevent us from reaching theirs. Additionally, considering earth is only one planet in our system and there are millions and millions of other solar systems, it seems very egotistical and small-minded to believe we are the only life form.

I also observe nature and marvel at its consistency and the order in the universe. Things as basic as the changing of the seasons and the sun rising each day lead me to the belief that all this is not an accident.

Seemingly, our life essence is having a human experience which is directed by a greater consciousness beyond our comprehension. I hope and believe that one of the things we are to learn is the ability of our mind to direct our bodies and our lives. We are developing and learning the capacity of our life essence.

Another thing I hope and believe is we exist to learn compassion and understand that we are all going through this human experience together. We are only one group, humanity, sharing this earth in the same time period.

We are one people and each is living to understand his or her individual purpose and meaning.

Consider this book as a resource for some thoughts for you to play with and evaluate their place in your human experience. I offer this book as if I am a high school track coach. You have to decide to come out for the team. I can only offer some ideas to help you create an appropriate strategy as you develop your abilities to run the race you choose. As you get into the starting blocks and the starter shouts: "Runners take your mark!", "Get set!", and "BANG!", remember, you are the only person who can run your race using all your knowledge and abilities to finish where you want.

The ideas and concepts I have shared represent my map of the territory. For me they are true and I know the techniques work. I also realize my life is a work in progress and every new experience and idea allows for additional growth. I offer my map as a resource for you to evaluate and decide if any of my reality has value in creating your map. I only take responsibility for my life and only you are responsible for yours. Hopefully, what I have shared will support you and open passages through your walls.

In closing, I offer the following thoughts for your consideration.

I believe there is a greater consciousness which the word God represents. I wish you God's blessings.

I hope you are successful in identifying your goals, dreams, and ideals and allow them to guide your journey.

We are one people and we must be compassionate and understanding of our oneness. Sharing with others expands our lives.

Keep a childlike curiosity about life. Maintain an alertness and openness to new thoughts and never let your walls restrict you from becoming the person you choose to be.

God grant me the serenity
to accept the things
I cannot change,
the courage to change
the things I can,
and the wisdom to know the difference.

Be well and enjoy your journey

WALLS as a tool for mentoring

The book *WALLS* is an effective tool to use as the focal point for interactive discussions. These discussions allow the participants to explore some basic essential elements of being responsible for their lives and creating the future they desire. The book is not designed to give answers: rather, it assists people in formulating better questions consistent with their own lives. As they explore possibilities they will discover their own answers to their own questions.

The book provides a model or map that keeps the discussions focused on the issues. Another benefit of using the book is that it allows the participants to discuss the issues on a conversational level and they do not have to share any specific personal information about their own life.

For additional thoughts on using the book *WALLS* for mentoring or to get information on book pricing for organizations using the book for mentoring please call Callahan Associates at 1-800-488-7618.

The following are some suggestions you can consider for using the *WALLS* interactive discussions as the basis for mentoring:

Each participant receives their own copy of *WALLS*. This allows to participants to read the book at their own pace and review the material whenever they choose. Reading is not a requirement for participating in these discussions because only one person needs to read in order for the book to provide the focal point for the discussion. People who have difficulty reading bring a different perspective and insights to the discussion. Having their own copy establishes the expectation that they will soon learn to read.

Establish a time frame for the discussions. Between one and two hours is an appropriate length for each session. Marathon sessions tend to get out of control and are less effective.

Have the discussions on a consistent basis. This allows the participants time to consider the issues discussed. Start each session with a short review of the previous session.

Clearly identify the objective for the discussions. Example:
The objective is to participate in a discussion with the intention of expanding my perspective and choices by exploring new possibilities.